THINKING, FEELING, BEHAVING

An Emotional Education Curriculum for Adolescents

GRADES 7-12

ANN VERNON

RESEARCH PRESS
2612 North Mattis Avenue
Champaign, Illinois 61821

CONTENTS

PROBLEM SOLVING/DECISION MAKING

INTERPERSONAL RELATIONSHIPS

Grades 11–12

SELF-ACCEPTANCE

FEELINGS

BELIEFS AND BEHAVIOR

FOREWORD

Albert Ellis claims to have invented Rational-Emotive Therapy (RET) in elementary school as a way to cope with his own feelings about being a latchkey child and to have reinvented it in his early 20s as a means to overcome his intense shyness. Later on, in the 1960s, Ellis began to use RET in his professional practice with individuals and couples. In doing so, he noted two interesting things: First, his sex and marital therapy with couples involved more direct teaching than did his more psychoanalytically oriented individual practice. And, second, his sex and marital therapy clients improved much faster than his individual clients.

Even though RET began as a psychotherapy intended for use with adults, it has always had a psychoeducational emphasis. Not only does RET involve active teaching of principles and ideas, it also can be understood even by young children and readily used outside of the therapeutic setting to overcome emotional problems.

In the present volume and its companion volume for children, Ann Vernon has extended the early work of Ellis and other practitioners of RET to create the most detailed, explicit, and comprehensive lesson plans currently available for teaching RET principles. Importantly, the exercises contained here are based on the results of many research studies into the effects of RET in the educational area. The activities are appropriate for youngsters in regular classes; in addition, they will be especially useful in working with students already identified as having emotional problems.

Finally, research suggests that efforts to help students stay emotionally healthy are best begun long before problems arise. Psychotherapists and counselors working with children and adolescents individually or in groups will no doubt find the activities contained here very helpful. My greatest hope for this volume and its companion, however, is that they will be widely applied in the classroom as a effort toward such primary prevention.

Raymond DiGiuseppe
Institute for Rational-Emotive Therapy

ACKNOWLEDGMENTS

This book and its companion volume, *Thinking, Feeling, Behaving: An Emotional Education Curriculum for Children,* are the result of years of training and practicing Rational-Emotive Therapy (RET). Thanks for the original impetus go naturally to Dr. Albert Ellis, founder of RET and Director of the Institute for Rational-Emotive Therapy.

It was at the Institute where I was first introduced to the concept of rational-emotive education in a presentation by Dr. Virginia Waters. I would like to thank Dr. Waters and also Dr. Richard Wessler, who offered to critique my first efforts to create emotional education activities for young people, collected in *Help Yourself to a Healthier You* (Minneapolis: Burgess, 1989).

With the encouragement of Dr. Ray DiGiuseppe, I undertook further RET training. I would like to thank him for his support, as well as for referring me to Maria Columbo, an elementary school teacher in Canton, Ohio, who collaborated on lesson objectives and contributed activities in the interpersonal relationships and problem-solving/decision-making sections of the volume for children. My gratitude goes to all of these people for their contributions to a program I think will have a positive influence on the lives of many young people.

INTRODUCTION

We live in a time marked by rapid change. All of us are faced with the challenge of adjusting to a world that is no longer as predictable and secure as it once was, and, for children, growing up is more difficult than ever before. Although many young people are able to master these life challenges, childhood stress is at epidemic proportions—and childhood depression and suicide are also on the increase. These problems make a dramatic statement about how difficult it is for many young people to cope with contemporary issues as well as with the typical milestones that characterize childhood development.

Given these realities, it is imperative that we address the social and emotional development of our children. Parents must necessarily shoulder much of this burden, but schools can also encourage such learning. Our responsibilities as educators and counselors include not only providing young people with knowledge and facts, but also teaching them the survival skills they will need to cope successfully with modern-day living.

An Emotional Health Curriculum

The purpose of this volume and its companion, *Thinking, Feeling, Behaving: An Emotional Education Curriculum for Children,* is to provide educators, counselors, school psychologists, social workers, and others working in the schools with a comprehensive curriculum to help youngsters learn positive mental health concepts. Each volume contains a total of 90 activities, field tested, arranged by grade levels, and grouped into the following topic areas: Self-Acceptance, Feelings, Beliefs and Behavior, Problem Solving/ Decision Making, and Interpersonal Relationships.

Several features distinguish this curriculum from other efforts to teach mental health concepts. First, lessons are sequential in nature and developmentally appropriate for the grade levels specified. The two volumes used together thus provide an integrated program for students in grades 1–12. This approach, in which activities for children at different developmental levels build upon previous program experiences, can be expected to have an effect well beyond that of less systematic efforts.

Next, each activity seeks to achieve a specific objective. These objectives, plainly stated, offer guidance in what concepts to stress and what outcomes to expect. In addition, each activity contains both content and personalization discussion questions that may be expanded upon, if desired. Content questions ensure mastery of concepts, whereas personalization questions encourage students to apply the concepts they learn. This personalization component is critical because it helps to move students from intellectualization about what they learn to understanding of how such learning can enable them to cope more positively with the challenges of growing up. Finally, student involvement characterizes all activities, with participants deducing understandings from simulation games, role playing, stories, written activities, brainstorming, and art activities.

Perhaps the most important feature of the curriculum concerns the fact that its content is strongly based on the theoretical principles of Rational-Emotive Therapy (RET), a system uniquely suited to emotional education.

Foundations of Rational-Emotive Therapy

Because only a brief overview is possible here, readers unfamiliar with RET are encouraged to study further the references listed at the end of this introduction. However, the following discussion will attempt to describe briefly the basic premises of the theory.

Based on the work of Albert Ellis, founder of the Institute for Rational-Emotive Therapy in New York, RET is a counseling intervention generally based on the assumption that emotional problems result from faulty thinking about events rather than from events themselves. As such, it involves a cognitive-emotive-behavioral system. This idea is illustrated by the A–B–C theory of emotional disturbance, where A is an activating event, B are beliefs about the event, and C is the emotional and behavioral consequence.

$$A \longrightarrow B \longrightarrow C$$

| Activating Event | Beliefs | Consequence |

Many people feel that activating events cause consequences. However, RET thinking holds that beliefs about the event intervene and are critical in determining consequences. If beliefs are rational, they result in moderate emotions that enable people to act constructively and achieve their goals. In contrast, irrational beliefs lead to disturbed emotions such as anger, anxiety, or depression, thus making goal attainment difficult.

The core construct of RET is that emotional upset stems from three major irrational beliefs.

1. I must do well and win approval for my performances, or else I rate as a rotten person.

2. Others must treat me considerately and kindly in precisely the way I want them to treat me; if they don't, society and the universe should severely blame, damn, and punish them for their inconsiderateness.

3. Conditions under which I live must get arranged so that I get practically everything I want comfortably, quickly, and easily, and get virtually nothing that I don't want. (Ellis, 1980, pp. 5–7)

These irrational beliefs result in some very nonproductive feelings and attitudes.

1. Worthlessness ("I am a worthless person if I don't do as well and win as much approval as I must.")

2. Awfulizing ("It is awful, terrible, or horrible that I am not doing as I must.")

3. I-can't-stand-it-itis ("I can't stand, can't bear the things that are happening to me that must not happen!") (Ellis, 1980, p. 8)

The "must" that characterizes these feelings and attitudes translates into the following kinds of statements, easily recognizable to anyone who works with adolescents.

It would be awful if my peers didn't like me; I shouldn't make mistakes, especially social mistakes; It's my parents' fault I'm so miserable; I can't help it, that's just the way I am and I guess I'll always be this way; The world should be fair and just; It's awful when things do not go my way; It's better to avoid challenges than risk failure; I must conform to my peers; I can't stand to be criticized; Others should always be responsible. (Waters, 1981, p. 6)

Once such irrational beliefs are identified, the D and E of the A–B–C paradigm become operative. Disputing (D) means challenging irrational beliefs by questioning assumptions about the event. As disputing occurs and rational beliefs replace irrational ones, more moderate emotions (E) result.

To illustrate, take the example of Roseann, a 14-year-old girl who was in a constant turmoil about her relationships with friends. Roseann came to class one day complaining that her "best friend" hadn't sat by her at lunch (A—activating event) and expressed how angry and upset she was (C—emotional consequence). Roseann assumed that, if her friend didn't sit by her, it must mean her friend didn't like her anymore, that she (Roseann) was no good, and that she'd never have friends again (B—irrational beliefs). In addition, Roseann was demanding that her friend behave in a certain fashion and felt that, if she didn't, it was awful. In order to help Roseann deal with the problem, we would encourage her to challenge these irrational beliefs by disputation (D). To do so, we might ask the following questions to help her put the problem in perspective and feel less upset and angry (E).

1. Just because your friend sat with someone else, does that necessarily mean she doesn't like you or that she will never be your friend again?

2. Just because you are friends, is there a rule that says she can't sit with other people?

3. Why does the fact that she sat with someone else mean you're no good?

4. Suppose she sits with someone else tomorrow. What are your choices? Are you going to go around feeling miserable, or will you find someone else to sit with?

5. If you can't control what your friend does, what can you control?

Applications of RET with Young People

In 1970, the Institute for Rational Living opened The Living School, a private grade school in New York. The purpose of this school was to present RET concepts in addition to the typical elementary-level curriculum. During the course of the school's operation, it became evident that teachers could successfully help children improve their emotional health. Currently, RET is used extensively with children and adolescents, either on an individual basis, in the classroom, or in small-group counseling sessions.

There are several reasons an emotional education curriculum based on RET principles can be successful with school-age children. First, RET is educative in nature, its goal being to help people help themselves by teaching them positive mental health concepts. More importantly, the core irrational beliefs RET attempts to modify relate to many of the basic problems faced by young people today: equating self-worth with performance and therefore never feeling good about oneself; awfulizing about events, then reacting in self-defeating ways (for example, by abusing alcohol or drugs); overgeneralizing and losing perspective on problems, then reacting impulsively (perhaps even by committing suicide). In addition, many young people seem to be caught up in the irrational attitude that things should come easily; this perspective results in impatience about having to work hard and set long-term goals. Finally, unless young people are taught to change these negative feelings by changing their thoughts, efforts at prevention or remediation will be superficial. A central goal of RET is to help people successfully alter these thoughts.

The activities in this volume address core irrational concepts through a variety of participant activities and deductive questions. For example, Grades 9–10 Beliefs and Behavior Activity 1 (Copping Out) attempts to combat the belief adolescents frequently hold that other people are responsible for outcomes. Specifically, students establish a definition of cop-out behavior and, through brainstorming, are invited to share personal examples of such behaviors. Discussion about the effects of cop-out behavior completes the activity. Another commonly held irrational belief is that individuals have no control over themselves or events—that things are the way they are and will always be that way. In Grades 7–8 Problem-Solving/Decision-Making Activity 3 (What Can You Control?), students are asked to respond to several stimulus situations on a continuum ranging from total control to no control. Discussion centers around understanding the concept of control and disputing the assumption that nothing can ever change.

Using Program Materials

In recent years, increasing interest has been shown toward developing preventative delivery systems designed to minimize or eliminate potential problems youngsters may experience. As noted by Bernard and Joyce (1984), the goal of preventative mental health programs is to facilitate the social and emotional growth of children by developing interpersonal relationship skills, enhancing self-esteem, improving problem-solving and decision-making strategies, developing a flexible outlook on life, acquiring a personal value system, and learning communication skills. Insofar as is possible, it is recommended that program activities be used in a preventative way, before problems in these areas arise. The program also lends itself to remediative efforts, however, and can be used successfully to intervene with youngsters who are having specific adjustment problems.

Activities are primarily intended to be used in classroom or small-group counseling settings. With minor adaptations, they can also be used in individual counseling sessions. Other changes may be required to ensure that activities are appropriate for particular situations and groups; these alterations are encouraged, as is the creation of new activities.

Each activity contains two main parts: a stimulus activity and discussion. At the beginning of the session, it is a good idea to explain the lesson's objective, particularly for older youngsters. Stimulus activities are generally designed to last 15–20 minutes so that, in the confines of the typical 50-minute class, sufficient time can be devoted to discussion. The discussion will allow students to learn specific skills; be introspective about particular concepts; and gain insights to help them learn more about themselves, their relationships, their behaviors, and their feelings. Since discussion is a critical element of the activities, whenever possible it is a good idea to have students seated in a circle.

Many of the activities encourage students to look at themselves and to share and learn from classmates with regard to emotional adjustment. It is therefore imperative that an atmosphere of trust and group cohesion be established. If the appropriate atmosphere exists, students often welcome the opportunity to share. However, if children seem uncomfortable sharing something personal, allow them to "pass." Don't force them to participate in discussion. Just hearing the other participants share and discuss will be a learning experience and will help normalize feelings and thoughts youngsters may have had but were simply reluctant to bring up.

It is also important that certain ground rules be established early on. Such rules can help to ensure that youngsters respect one another's opinions and expressions, understand that discussion of a personal nature is confidential and should stay within the group, and know that they have a choice whether or not they share personal information about themselves. Consistently enforcing these ground rules will provide children with a "safe space" to express their feelings and will encourage them to feel free to learn these important concepts.

For Further Information

Bernard, M.E., & Joyce, M.R. (1984). *Rational-Emotive Therapy with children and adolescents: Theory, treatment strategies, preventative methods.* New York: Wiley.

Dryden, W., & Trower, P. (Eds.). (1986). *Rational-Emotive Therapy: Recent developments in theory and practice.* Bristol, England: Institute for Rational-Emotive Therapy.

Ellis, A. (1962). *Reason and emotion in psychotherapy.* New York: Lyle Stuart.

Ellis, A. (1971a). *Growth through reason.* North Hollywood, CA: Wilshire.

Ellis, A. (1971b). *Humanistic psychotherapy.* New York: Crown.

Ellis, A. (1980). An overview of the clinical theory of Rational-Emotive Therapy. In R. Grieger & J. Byrd (Eds.), *Rational-Emotive Therapy: A skills-based approach.* New York: Van Nostrand.

Ellis, A., & Bernard, M.E. (1983). *Rational-emotive approaches to the problems of childhood.* New York: Plenum.

Ellis, A., & Grieger, R. (1977). *Handbook of Rational-Emotive Therapy.* New York: Springer.

Ellis, A., & Whitely, J.M. (1979). *Theoretical and empirical foundations of Rational-Emotive Therapy.* Monterey, CA: Brooks/Cole.

Grieger, R., & Boyd, J. (1980). *Rational-Emotive Therapy: A skills-based approach.* New York: Van Nostrand.

Vernon, A. (1983). Rational-emotive education. In A. Ellis & M. Bernard (Eds.), *Rational-emotive approaches to the problems of childhood.* New York: Plenum.

Walen, S.R., DiGiuseppe, R.A., & Wessler, R.L. (1980). *A practitioner's guide to Rational-Emotive Therapy.* New York: Oxford.

Waters, V. (1981). *The Living School.* New York: Institute for Rational Living.

Wessler, R.A., & Wessler, R.L. (1983). *The principles and practice of Rational-Emotive Therapy.* San Francisco: Jossey-Bass.

GRADES

7-8

SELF-ACCEPTANCE

I Dare You

Objective

To recognize the relationship between self-acceptance, behavior, and feelings

Materials

None

Procedure

1. Ask students how many of them have ever done something only because someone else dared them to do it. Indicate that you will be discussing the relationship between their behavior, their feelings, and what they think of themselves in situations in which they have been dared to do something.
2. Tell them a story about Tony: Tony's friends drew a picture of a pig and labeled it with the school principal's name. Then they dared Tony to go into the principal's office and put the picture on the desk. Tony did it because he felt he had to.

Discussion

Content Questions

1. How do you suppose Tony felt when his friends dared him to put the picture on the principal's desk?
2. What do you think would have happened if he had said no?
3. How do you think he felt about doing what he did?

Personalization Questions

1. Have you ever been in a situation like this? Share examples.
2. How did you feel about your behavior if you took the dare? How did you feel about your behavior if you didn't take the dare?
3. Do you think you'd feel better about yourself if you didn't take the dare or if you did? What factors are important to consider in situations like this?
4. Can you explain the connections between your behavior, your feelings, and your own self-acceptance in situations like this?

To the Leader

It is important for students to realize that, if they don't want to do something but do it anyway, they will probably not feel as good about themselves as if they had resisted.

Circles of Self

Objective

To identify the physical, intellectual, spiritual, emotional, and social aspects of self

Materials

Circles of Self Worksheets (Handout 1); pens or pencils as needed

Procedure

1. Distribute the Circles of Self Worksheets (Handout 1) and explain that the focus of the lesson will be on the issue of identity. One's identity includes various aspects: physical, intellectual, spiritual, emotional, and social.

2. Instruct students to describe themselves by identifying three words or phrases for each of the categories on the worksheet. For example, in the *social* category, a student might put the words *outgoing, likes people,* etc.

3. Once the circles are completed, ask students to share the words or phrases from any two categories with a partner.

Discussion

Content Questions

1. How difficult was it to think of words or phrases to describe yourself?

2. If you don't feel as comfortable with one category as you do the others, what does that say about you as a person?

3. Is there a relationship between these categories? For example, if you think you have intellectual strengths, do you also feel better emotionally? What are the connections for you?

4. If you were trying to explain to someone who you are, how would you do it?

To the Leader

Help students recognize that all of these aspects make up one's identity and, just because students may feel strong or weak in one area, this shouldn't influence their attitudes about who they are as a whole.

Circles of Self Worksheet

Directions: Identify three words or phrases in each category that tell something about you.

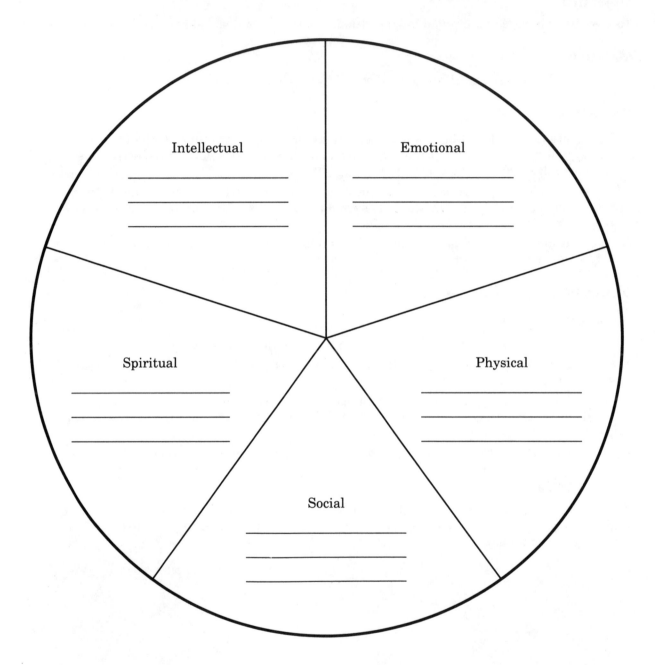

Who Counts?

Objective

To learn the importance of self-acceptance despite the risk of others' disapproval

Materials

Paper and pencils as needed

Procedure

1. Introduce the lesson by asking students if they have ever done something they felt good about but knew that their friends would laugh at or criticize. Ask for several examples.

2. Ask students to listen to the following situations and be prepared to finish the scenarios by writing a response to each.

   > Susan is smart and can get good grades without trying, but if she does raise her hand to answer all the time, finish early, or help others out, kids . . .

   > Ted is really a good actor, but most of his friends are athletic. He's thinking of not trying out for the school play because . . .

   > Debbie knows the difference between right and wrong, but she wants to fit in, too. When her friends encourage her to make fun of the teacher, she does it because . . .

   > Don knows that cheating is wrong, but when the guys ask him to let them look over his shoulder during a test, he does it because . . .

3. Invite students to share examples of responses to each scenario.

Discussion

Content Questions

1. Were any of these situations familiar to you? Share examples.

Personalization Questions

1. What have you done in situations of this nature?
2. How do you feel about yourself if you do something you know is wrong or something with which you aren't comfortable?
3. Do you think it is better to risk others' disapproval and feel good about yourself and your decisions or to do what your friends want?

To the Leader

Emphasizing the relationship between feelings toward self and risking others' disapproval is extremely important for students at this age, when peer pressure is so prevalent.

Who's in Charge?

Objective

To recognize the degree of personal control over events

Materials

Who's in Charge Worksheets (Handout 2); pens or pencils as needed

Procedure

1. Introduce the activity by asking students to raise their hands if they feel as though they have control over things that happen in their lives.
2. Distribute a Who's in Charge Worksheet (Handout 2) to each student. Have students read each situation and mark the degree of control they feel they have over it.

Discussion

Content Questions

1. Did you mark any items as being your fault only? Share examples.
2. Did you mark any items as being others' fault only? Share examples.

Personalization Questions

1. How much personal control do you think you have over what happens to you?
2. If you don't think you have much, is there anything you can do about it?
3. How much control do you think is desirable?

To the Leader

It is important for students to recognize that they have a lot more personal control than they realize. Taking responsibility for events will result in a greater sense of personal power.

Who's in Charge Worksheet

Directions: Read each of the situations and put a mark on the continuum to indicate the degree to which you feel you or others are in charge of what happens.

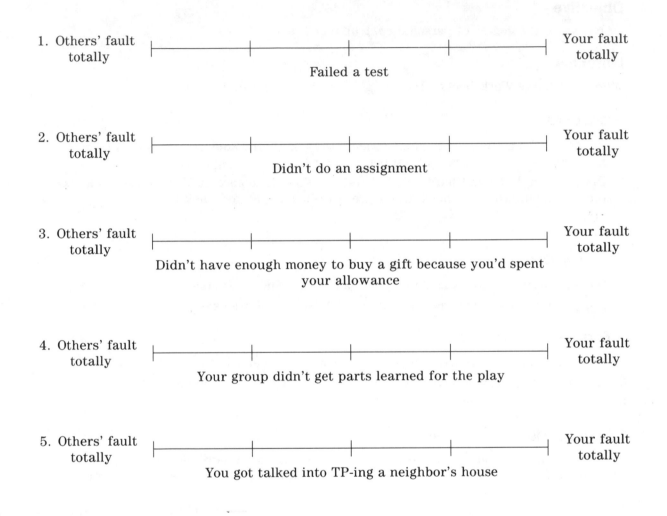

1. Others' fault totally ⊢————————————————————⊣ Your fault totally
   Failed a test

2. Others' fault totally ⊢————————————————————⊣ Your fault totally
   Didn't do an assignment

3. Others' fault totally ⊢————————————————————⊣ Your fault totally
   Didn't have enough money to buy a gift because you'd spent your allowance

4. Others' fault totally ⊢————————————————————⊣ Your fault totally
   Your group didn't get parts learned for the play

5. Others' fault totally ⊢————————————————————⊣ Your fault totally
   You got talked into TP-ing a neighbor's house

I Want, I Need

Objective

To distinguish between personal wants and needs

Materials

Paper and pencils as needed

Procedure

1. Write the words *want* and *need* in two columns on the chalkboard. Ask students to give some random examples of things they need and things they want.

2. After several examples have been given, explain that a need is something that we have to have, such as food or water, and a want is a desire. Indicate that we frequently say we need something when actually we only want it. Most needs are actually wants.

3. Invite students to make a list of five things they think are needs and five things they think are wants. Have them share lists with a partner.

Discussion

Content Questions

1. What is the difference between a need and a want?
2. Are some of the things you have listed as needs actually wants?

Personalization Questions

1. What did you learn about your own personal needs and wants?
2. Which do you have more of—needs or wants? What are the implications of having more of one or the other?

To the Leader

This distinction is an important one. If students can recognize the difference between needs and wants, they may be able to put some of their desires and demands in better perspective.

I'm Not What I Do

Objective

To recognize that one's worth as a person is not connected to what one does

Materials

Ten index cards per student; masking tape

Procedure

1. Distribute the index cards and ask students to write down some examples of performances they have given in the past few months. Examples would include playing in a recital, giving a speech, taking a test, doing the dishes, performing in a play, finishing a chore, etc.
2. Ask for two students to volunteer to take each of their cards and tape them on their arms, legs, or other parts of their bodies. Ask the group how many of them know the first volunteer. Read each card and tear it off the student as it is read. When all cards are off, ask the other students if the person is still the same person without his or her performances.
3. Follow the same procedure with the other volunteer.

Discussion

Content Questions

1. Once the volunteers were stripped of their performances, were they still the same people?
2. Does what someone do change who he or she is as a person?
3. What is the connection between who one is and what one does?

Personalization Questions

1. Do you think the performances you wrote down change who you are as a person?
2. Have you ever felt bad about yourself because you didn't do something well? Share examples. After experiencing this lesson, would you still feel bad about yourself?

To the Leader

Students can realize that, even if they perform extremely well or extremely poorly, they are still worthwhile. Stress the fact that who one is involves more than what one does.

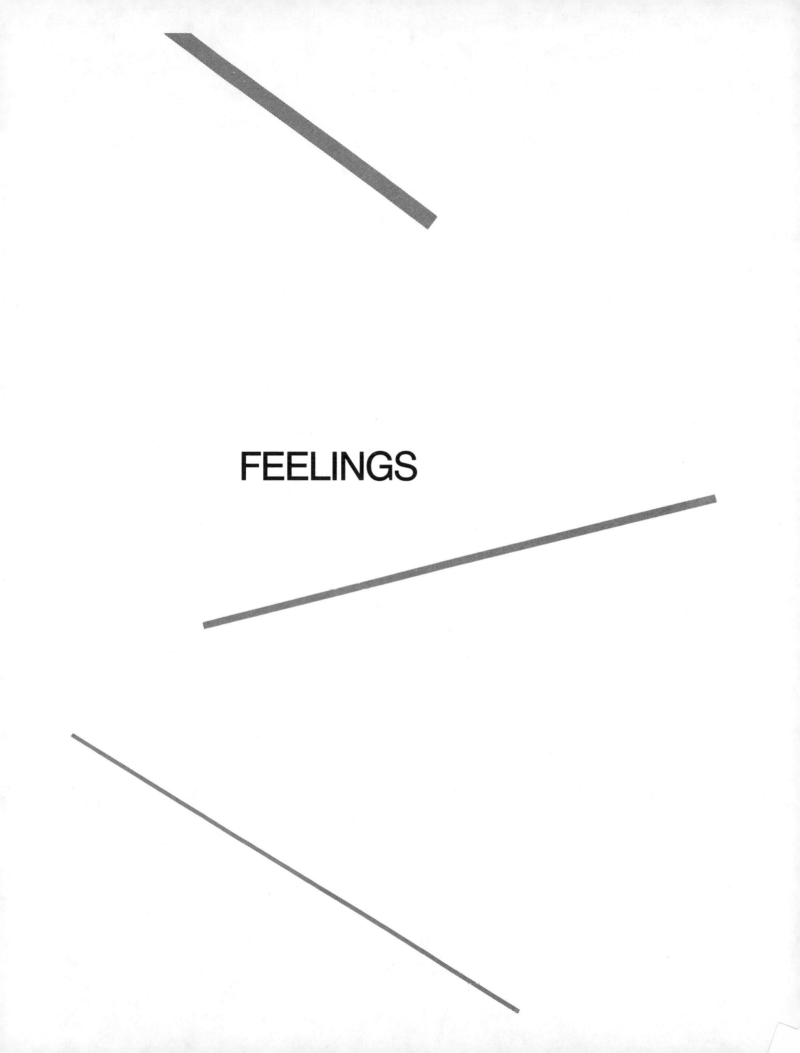

FEELINGS

Who's Responsible for Feelings?

Objective

To recognize that others aren't responsible for our unhappiness

Materials

Paper and pencils as needed

Procedure

1. Discuss what it means to be disappointed and ask students to make a list of at least three disappointing events they have experienced recently. Examples might include not getting invited to someone's house, having to go somewhere you don't want to go, or getting a low grade on an assignment.

2. Next ask students to indicate how they responded to the disappointment: Did they yell, cry, argue, blame someone else, or make some other response?

3. Ask them to identify who they think is to blame for their unhappiness or their disappointment—themselves or someone else?

4. Invite students to share some examples of situations, reactions, and who they think is to blame.

5. Illustrate that unhappy feelings come from our thoughts by taking one example situation and identifying the thoughts surrounding it. For example, if a student is upset about getting a bad grade on a test, he or she would likely be saying or thinking something like the following.

    The test was too hard.

    It shouldn't been that hard.

    I shouldn't have to study for tests.

    This situation is unfair.

6. Discuss whether or not students really have to think and feel this way. Show that the same student might feel entirely different if he or she thought the following.

    I wish I'd studied harder.

    I could have asked questions to help me understand.

    It's too bad I got a bad grade, but I'll do better next time.

    I'm not what I do—I'm still OK.

Discussion

Content Questions

1. Who is usually to blame for your disappointment—you or someone else?

2. Is it really possible for someone else to be responsible for your unhappiness or disappointment?

3. Where do disappointed or unhappy feelings come from?

1. What can you do when you find yourself blaming someone else for your unhappiness?

2. Who is usually more in charge of your feelings—you or someone else? If you think someone else is, how can they really be responsible for your feelings?

To the Leader

By helping students identify what they are telling themselves about an unhappy situation, you can help them see that they are responsible for their feelings—no one else is to blame.

Talk to Yourself

Objective

To learn to use self-talk for emotional control

Materials

Talk to Yourself Situations Lists (Handout 3); pens or pencils as needed

Procedure

1. Ask students if they have ever talked to themselves when they have some sort of a problem. For instance, if they don't get an *A* on a test, do they say to themselves that they are stupid and that they can never do anything right?

2. Next ask students if they have ever talked to a friend who had a similar problem. Do they say the same things to the friend, or do they suggest the grade might just mean the person should study more and that he or she will probably do better next time? In other words, are the messages the same?

3. Instruct students to find partners, then distribute a copy of the Talk to Yourself Situations List (Handout 3) to each pair. Together, students are to identify what they would say to themselves and what they would say to a friend about each situation.

4. Invite students to share examples of self-talk and other talk for several of the situations.

Discussion

Content Questions

1. Was your self-talk and other talk the same? What were the similarities and differences?

2. Which was easier to identify—what you would tend to say to yourself or to others?

3. Which kind of talk makes more sense—the kind you give to yourself or to others?

Personalization Questions

1. Do you use self-talk? When you do, is it usually helpful, or are you sometimes too hard on yourself or too narrow in your thinking?

2. What do you think you can do the next time you catch yourself being too negative in your self-talk?

To the Leader

Frequently, we are too critical or not objective enough in our self-talk, whereas our comments to a friend would be much more supportive. It is important to begin to change negative self-talk because such talk can result in negative feelings.

Talk to Yourself Situations List

Directions: Read each of the situations and identify what you might say to yourself if this problem occurred and what you might say to a friend with the same problem.

1. Got an *F* on a paper.

Self-talk _____

Other talk _____

2. Didn't get asked to the dance.

Self-talk _____

Other talk _____

3. Got complimented on a new outfit.

Self-talk _____

Other talk _____

4. Have to get glasses.

Self-talk _____

Other talk _____

5. Got asked to a party and don't like the person giving it.

Self-talk _____

Other talk _____

I Can, I Can't

Objective

To develop the ability to change "I can't help how I feel" language to "I can help how I feel" language

Materials

I Can, I Can't Situations Lists (Handout 4)

Procedure

1. Ask students to find a partner. Distribute the I Can, I Can't Situations List (Handout 4) to each person.
2. Partners are to identify themselves as A or B. A is to read one situation to B, and B is to say loudly, "I can't." Then B reads the next situation, and A responds, "I can't." Partners continue until the entire list has been read.

Discussion

Content Questions

1. What effect did it have on you when your partner kept saying, "I can't?"
2. Can you think of other responses that you might have made?
3. When people say, "I can't," do you think they really can't?

Personalization Questions

1. Do you ever say, "I can't" and not really mean it?
2. If you feel bad and say, "I can't help it," do you think what you're saying is true? Have you had any experiences like this?
3. Do you think you can or can't control your feelings?

To the Leader

In processing this activity, stress the fact that we readily tend to think we can't do something when, in actuality, we can in most situations control our feelings, thoughts, and behaviors.

HANDOUT 4

I Can, I Can't Situations List

Directions: Partners identify themselves as A or B. A reads the first statement to B, and B says, "I can't." Then B reads the next statement to A, and A says, "I can't." Continue until all statements have been read.

1. Stop crying!

2. Stop eating like a pig.

3. Stop being so picky.

4. Stop feeling sorry for yourself.

5. Stop putting yourself down.

6. Stop moping around.

7. Stop blaming others for your problems.

8. Stop being so cheerful . . . it makes us feel bad.

Avoiding Anger

Objective

To learn that anger can be managed or avoided

Materials

Paper and pencils as needed

Procedure

1. Discuss the definition of anger and invite students to identify a recent situation that resulted in angry feelings. Ask them to identify what the situation was and why the situation resulted in anger.

2. Divide students into small groups (4–6 participants) to share their situations. Ask them to avoid using names of any classmates that might have been involved. Allow about 10 minutes for sharing, then reassemble the entire group for discussion.

Discussion

Content Questions

1. Are the situations that anger you similar to situations that anger others?

2. Do you think others would have gotten angry about your situation? Why do you think something angers one person and not another?

3. Are the reasons for your anger similar to the reasons given by others? (Share common themes around which anger is centered, such as being thwarted, put down, not having things go your way, etc.)

4. In the situations identified, did you have to feel angry? What else could you have felt?

Personalization Questions

1. Would you rather feel angry, or would you rather not? Is anger a positive feeling for you?

2. Next time you feel angry and decide you'd rather not be, what can you do about it?

To the Leader

It is important for students to see that anger is a choice. Draw from Grades 7–8 Feelings Activity 2 (Talk to Yourself) and emphasize that self-talk can be used to control or avoid anger.

Chain Reactions

Objective

To recognize the chain effect of negative emotions

Materials

A paper chain with the words *mad, inferior,* and *guilty* written on the first three loops. The chain should have at least 12 more loops.

Procedure

1. Show the paper chain and discuss the concept of a chain reaction, in which one event triggers others or, in this case, one situation triggers a chain of emotions.

2. Reiterate the point that thoughts control feelings and ask students to imagine they have just found out they have not been invited to a party. Ask them what thoughts they might be having if they were feeling *mad* (the word written on the first link). Elicit such thoughts as "It's terrible that I'm not invited," "I must be a real jerk," etc.

3. Next ask students to imagine that, after feeling mad, they have the subsequent thought "If only I were more popular." Explain that having this thought contributes to feeling *inferior* (the word on the next link). Then ask students to imagine that thinking they are inferior results in their having yet another thought, beginning "If only I'd said . . . " Point out that this thought contributes to feeling *guilty* (the final word written on the chain).

4. As a group, try to identify another sequence involving an event, initial thoughts and feelings about that event, and subsequent thoughts and feelings. Write this sequence on the chain. Do several examples to demonstrate the concept.

5. Take the same chain and try reversing the thoughts. For example, with regard to not being invited to a party, ask students how they might feel if they thought, "So what, I'm busy that night anyway." Discuss how this initial thought would influence the entire chain.

Discussion

Content Questions

1. As demonstrated by this activity, what is the connection between events, thoughts, and feelings?

2. Do you think that it is common to have a chain reaction of negative thoughts and feelings?

3. What can be done to break negative cycles?

Personalization Questions

1. Have you experienced a negative chain reaction before?

2. If you have experienced one, what was the result? Did it go on for a long time? How did you break the cycle?

3. Was it helpful to continue to think negative thoughts and feelings?

To the Leader

Awareness of the chain reaction tendency is important, as is the knowledge that this cycle can be brought under control by changing one's thoughts and, subsequently, one's feelings. Refer to Grades 7–8 Feelings Activities 2 and 4 (Talk to Yourself and Avoiding Anger) for additional reinforcement of concepts related to this activity.

The ABC's

Objective

To analyze emotional hurt according to the ABC theory

Materials

Paper and pencils as needed

Procedure

1. Ask students to think of one upsetting experience that has occurred within the past month or so. Ask for a volunteer to share an experience.

2. Use the volunteer's experience to illustrate the ABC model. Suppose, for example, the volunteer says he or she did not make the basketball team. Not being invited becomes the A (the event or occurrence).

$$A \longrightarrow B \longrightarrow C$$

Ask the volunteer to evaluate the feelings associated with the situation (for example, being upset). The feelings are the C. Point out that, when we have a C, we usually also have a behavior (such as sulking). Explain that, although we might think A's (events) cause C's (feelings and actions), we know this can't be true because people can react very differently to the same events. The reason for this difference is that we have B's, or beliefs, about the event. Ask the volunteer to identify the beliefs surrounding the event (perhaps that he or she is worthless or will never be a success at anything).

3. Illustrate the ABC model with other situations students are willing to share. Invite them to speculate on how their C's (feelings and actions) would be different if they were able to change their B's (beliefs).

Discussion

Content Questions

1. Where do feelings come from?
2. If you change your beliefs, what happens to your feelings?
3. Do two people necessarily feel the same about a situation? Why or why not?

Personalization Questions

1. Have you ever changed your feelings by changing your thoughts about an event? Share examples.
2. How can you apply the information you learned today to future situations?

To the Leader

For more information on the ABC theory, see the discussion and reference list provided in the Introduction.

BELIEFS AND BEHAVIOR

Wants and Needs

Objective

To learn to recognize the difference between wants and needs

Materials

12 slips of paper per student; pens or pencils as needed

Procedure

1. Distribute 12 slips of paper to each student. Ask students to brainstorm quickly 10 things they either want or need and write these items on the separate slips of paper. Next students are to take the two additional slips of paper and write *wants* on one and *needs* on the other. They are then to categorize the other slips according to these two groups.

2. Ask students to define the terms *want* and *need*. Point out that a need is something one must have in order to survive. Needs may be physical, such as food, clothing, or shelter, or they may be emotional, such as security, love, and a sense of belonging to a family or group. A want is something that would make one more comfortable or life easier but that isn't necessary for survival.

3. After students have considered the definitions, invite them to change the items in each of their groups, if necessary. Instruct them to put a checkmark beside each item they switch.

4. Encourage students to share examples of their wants and needs.

Discussion

Content Questions

1. What is the difference between a want and a need?
2. Once you learned more about this difference, did you switch any of the items in your groupings?
3. Do you agree that all people need to have food, clothing, and shelter; feel security and love; and have a sense of belonging? What do these things mean to you?

Personalization Questions

1. Have you ever confused your own wants and needs, saying that you needed something when in fact you really only wanted it? What difference does it make when you think of something as a want rather than a need?
2. Have you ever needed something and been unable to get it? What effect did this situation have on you?
3. Have you ever wanted something and didn't get it? What effect did this situation have on you? Do you think you can always have everything you want?

To the Leader

Help students realize that people want and even need things to different degrees. At a basic level, we all need food, but some people need more than others, need certain kinds, etc. A fine line also exists between what one wants and what one really needs. Challenge students' thinking about these ideas.

What Will Happen to Me?

Objective

To learn to assess consequences of behavior with regard to one's own best interests

Materials

What Will Happen to Me Worksheet (Handout 5); pens or pencils as needed

Procedure

1. Introduce the concept of consequences and discuss the fact that a consequence is something that happens as a result of taking some action.

2. Distribute one What Will Happen to Me Worksheet (Handout 5) per student and have students identify consequences for the situations listed.

3. Make a list on the chalkboard of some of the consequences students were able to identify for each situation.

Discussion

Content Questions

1. Was it difficult to think of consequences for these situations?

2. Is the seriousness of the consequences the same for each situation?

3. Did you think of more positive or negative consequences?

Personalization Questions

1. When you are in a particular situation, do you think of the consequences?

2. Can you identify a situation in which the consequences were positive because you thought through your behavior ahead of time? Is there an example of a time when the consequences were negative because you didn't think ahead?

3. How can you apply what you've learned about consequences to your own life?

To the Leader

Helping students assess the seriousness of consequences in light of their own best interests may help them to think before acting.

HANDOUT 5

What Will Happen to Me Worksheet

Directions: Read the situations and decide what the consequences might be.

1. You can't find a ride home after basketball practice and decide to walk because there is no phone available.

   Consequences:

2. One of your friends is having a party. Your dad says that you can go if the parents are going to be home. You say that they will be home but find out later that they aren't.

   Consequences:

3. You have a big science project due, but instead of working on it, you watch TV.

   Consequences:

4. Your friends dare you to steal some pop and candy from the neighborhood convenience store, and you do.

   Consequences:

5. You are taking a hard test and figure that you'll flunk it if you don't sneak a look in your book when the teacher isn't watching.

   Consequences:

6. You go to a movie your parents have forbidden you to see.

   Consequences:

7. You skip orchestra rehearsal so you can sleep later.

   Consequences:

8. You are at a friend's house and are offered some marijuana. You decide not to try it.

   Consequences:

What Will Happen to Others?

Objective

To learn to assess consequences of behavior in terms of impact on others

Materials

What Will Happen to Others Worksheets (Handout 6); pens or pencils as needed

Procedure

1. Review the concept of consequences presented in Grades 7–8 Beliefs and Behavior Activity 2 (What Will Happen to Me?) and emphasize the fact that consequences can affect both oneself and others. Distribute one What Will Happen to Others Worksheet (Handout 6) per student and instruct students to think about the effects of consequences on others.

2. On the chalkboard, list some of these consequences, then discuss.

Discussion

Content Questions

1. Was it difficult to think of what effect the consequences of your behavior would have on other people?

2. Were most of the consequences positive or negative?

Personalization Questions

1. When you do something, do you usually think about how that behavior will affect someone else? What happens if you don't think about this?

2. How can you apply what you learned today?

To the Leader

If students begin to think more about how their behavior affects others, they may be better able to choose appropriate actions.

HANDOUT 6

What Will Happen to Others Worksheet

Directions: Read each situation and decide what effect the consequences of your behavior would have on others.

1. One of your friends tells you a secret, and you tell someone else.

   Consequences:

2. You get kicked out of school for mouthing off to a teacher.

   Consequences:

3. You promise to help your grandmother do her grocery shopping because the bags are too heavy for her to carry. You never show up.

   Consequences:

4. You borrow your brother's letter jacket without asking and lose it at the game.

   Consequences:

5. Your mom asks you to mail some important letters. You forget and leave them in your backpack.

   Consequences:

6. You are mad at someone, so you tell a few other kids some things about that person that you weren't supposed to tell.

   Consequences:

7. You offer to show a new student around the school.

   Consequences:

8. You offer to help your sister with a project.

   Consequences:

Demand or Preference?

Objective

To learn to distinguish between demands and preferences

Materials

One deck of Demand or Preference Cards for each group of four students

Procedure

1. Divide the class into groups of four and explain that groups will be playing a game like Concentration. In this game, however, the objective is to distinguish between demands and preferences.

2. Discuss the definitions of the terms *demand* (a command that someone do something a certain way, an order, an expectation) and *preference* (when you would like something to happen or someone to do something, but you don't order it or necessarily expect it). For example, the statement "I'd like you to make your bed" is a preference, whereas the statement "You must be in by 9:00 p.m." is a demand.

3. Distribute the card decks. Students are to lay the cards face down, as in Concentration, putting six cards in each row. One player at a time turns over two cards and states whether the messages written on them are demands or preferences (or one of each). If the cards are the same in terms of content, and if correctly identified, they may be removed. If the player incorrectly identifies the cards, or if there is no match, the cards are turned back over. The leader acts as a judge if there is a question about the distinction between demands and preferences. The game ends when all cards have been removed.

Discussion

Content Questions

1. Was it difficult to distinguish between demands and preferences?
2. How do you explain the distinction between these two kinds of expression?

Personalization Questions

1. Do you usually make demands or express preferences? What about others with whom you interact?
2. How do you think it will help you to be able to distinguish between demands and preferences?
3. How can you apply what you have learned?

To the Leader

Students at this age often expect and demand that everything they want occur immediately. Help them to see that expressing preferences is important but that they can't necessarily expect everything they desire to come about.

Demand or Preference Cards

Directions: Copy each statement on two separate index cards to make one full deck. Make one deck for every four students.

I have to eat pizza once a week, or I can't stand it. *(demand)*

I wish I had more friends. *(preference)*

I'd like to see that movie. *(preference)*

I have to get an *A* on this test. *(demand)*

I like to stay up until 10:00 p.m. *(preference)*

I like eating pizza more than any other food. *(preference)*

If my parents don't let me go to the movies, I'll sneak out of the house. *(demand)*

I hope I get an *A* on the test. *(preference)*

If she says she won't be my friend, I'll die. *(demand)*

If I don't get to stay up until 10:00 p.m., I'll throw a fit. *(demand)*

I absolutely have to make the cheerleading squad. *(demand)*

I can't stand Mr. _____ . He'd better stop picking on me. *(demand)*

If I don't get science first period, I'll cut every day. *(demand)*

I hope I get picked to be a cheerleader. *(preference)*

I wish Mr. _____ wouldn't pick on me. *(preference)*

I hope I get first period science. *(preference)*

He'd better call me at 8:00 p.m., or I'll never speak to him again. *(demand)*

I hope he calls at 8:00 p.m. *(preference)*

Drop the Demands

Objective

To develop strategies for eliminating demanding behavior

Materials

Paper and pencils as needed

Procedure

1. Review the concept of being demanding by listing the following *shoulds* on the chalkboard:

   All students must dress neatly all the time, or they will be expelled.

   Parents have to let their kids do anything they want to do.

   I must get my way about everything.

   Teachers have to treat us fairly.

   I have to be perfect in everything I do.

2. Invite students to agree or disagree with the demands, pointing out that demands represent a category of irrational thinking because, although we may prefer that something be a certain way, there is usually no reason why it should be that way.

3. Ask students to write down three examples of demands that they have for themselves or others. Invite them to share.

4. Discuss the negative effects of being demanding. Point out that, if you think something has to be a certain way, then you will likely be upset and disappointed when it doesn't turn out as you want it to. Or, if you hold rigidly to demands, then it makes it hard for you to be flexible in your thinking, and you may end up with lots of negative emotions. For example, if you demand that someone call you to stay overnight but that person doesn't, you will probably be more upset than if you hadn't demanded to be invited.

5. Discuss the concept of eliminating demanding thoughts and behaviors by encouraging students to question their demands. Encourage them to ask themselves, "Who says things have to be a certain way?" "Is it reasonable to expect that the situation will go my way?" "Is it truly awful that things aren't working out the way I'd like them to?" etc. Use students' own examples to underline the point.

Discussion

Content Questions

1. Do you think the demands you identified are realistic?

2. When you asked yourself challenging questions, what did you learn about your demands?

3. What is the difference between preferring and demanding? Which is healthier?

Personalization Questions

1. What have you learned about being demanding?

2. If you think you are too demanding, do you want to change? If you do, how can you accomplish this change?

To the Leader

Show students how to talk to themselves about the unrealistic and negative nature of demands and emphasize the notion of preferring something as opposed to saying that it should or must be. These are difficult concepts; use lots of examples to get the point across.

Challenging Irrational Beliefs

Objective

To develop more flexible thinking by learning to challenge irrational beliefs

Materials

Challenging Irrational Beliefs Worksheets (Handout 7)

Procedure

1. Introduce the concept of flexibility in thinking by reviewing characteristics of irrational beliefs as presented in Grades 7–8 Beliefs and Behavior Activity 4 (Demand or Preference?) and Activity 5 (Drop the Demands).

2. Discuss the negative implications of irrational thinking: inflexibility in behavior towards others, unrealistically high expectations for self and others, demanding thoughts and behaviors, and negative emotions. Explain that irrational beliefs need to be challenged so that more flexible thinking can result.

3. Share the following as an example of challenging irrational thinking.

   ### Event

   You didn't make the team.

   ### Irrational beliefs

   I'm a failure.

   I'll never be any good at anything again.

   I should have tried harder.

   It's not fair—the coaches were biased.

   I'm giving up because this is too hard.

   ### Feelings

   Anger, defeat, discouragement

   ### Challenges

   Just because you didn't make the team, does that mean you are a failure in everything?

   Does it really mean you'll never be good at anything again? Even if you had tried harder, is it possible that you wouldn't have been selected?

   Just because you weren't selected, does that necessarily mean the coaches were biased? Is it possible that you do have some room for improvement—doesn't everyone?

   Aren't most things in life tough—what will you gain by giving up?

4. Discuss what occurs when you ask yourself challenging questions (in essence, you are replacing the irrational thoughts with more sensible ones).

5. Divide the class into two teams and give each team a copy of the Challenging Irrational Beliefs Worksheet (Handout 7). To begin, Player 1 from Team A reads the first item, and Player 1 from Team B states at least two irrational beliefs in response. (If this player fails to state two irrational beliefs, Player 2 on Team A may have a chance.) Next Player 2 from the opposing team states two challenges to the irrational beliefs. If that player fails to do so, Player 3 on the opposing team gets a chance, and so forth. The game continues until all items have been covered. One point is given for each correct response. The team with the most points accumulated after all the items have been read are the best challengers.

Discussion

Content Questions

1. What happened to the beliefs after you asked the challenging questions?
2. What problems did you have in asking the challenging questions?
3. What do you see as the value in asking challenging questions?

Personalization Questions

1. Have you ever challenged any of your own irrational beliefs? If so, what was the result?
2. If you haven't used challenges, is this technique something you think would be useful for you? (Invite students to share some examples of irrational beliefs they would like to challenge.)

To the Leader

Although the concept of challenging may be difficult, it is important to help students practice so that they can work on changing irrational thinking in daily interactions.

PROBLEM SOLVING/
DECISION MAKING

HANDOUT 7

Challenging Irrational Beliefs Worksheet

Directions: Player 1 from Team A reads the first item aloud. Player 1 from Team B must identify two irrational beliefs about the situation. Player 2 from Team A must then offer two challenges to these irrational beliefs. If any player gives an incorrect response, the opposing team gets a chance. Continue until all items have been read. Score one point for each correct response.

1. You have a chance to win the game for your team, and you miss the shot.

2. You don't get all *A*'s on your report card.

3. Your best friend moves away.

4. You've got the flu and have to miss the only school party of the year.

5. Cheerleading tryouts are tonight, and you're nervous.

6. A teacher blames you for something you didn't do.

7. You have tests in four subjects tomorrow.

8. Someone you have a crush on ignores you.

9. Your parents are getting a divorce.

10. A group of kids have been giving you a hard time about your clothes.

Staying Objective

Objective

To explore the effects of emotionalism on the problem-solving/decision-making process

Materials

Paper and pencils as needed

Procedure

1. Introduce the activity by brainstorming, as a group, some of the problems students this age need to solve or decisions they need to make. The list might include such things as whether to have a boyfriend or girlfriend, how to be accepted by peers, whether to drink or take drugs, whether or not to follow parents' rules, whether to study hard, etc.

2. Have students pair up and discuss the following situation.

> You have been good friends with a fellow student for the past 5 years. This person is very talented in athletics and music but is not very smart in history. Lately, this student has been hanging around with a different crowd and has made some rude remarks about you and some of your friends. The remarks have really upset you. Today this person asks to copy the history report you have been working on for over a week. What do you do?

3. Reassemble as a large group and share responses. Elicit comments on how emotions can complicate the decision-making process.

Discussion

Content Questions

1. How did the fact that you were upset about the relationship influence your decision as to what to do about the assignment? Would you have made the same decision if you hadn't been upset?

2. Do you think there would be any way to set aside your emotions and deal with the problem more objectively? If so, how?

Personalization Questions

1. Have you ever been forced to make a decision or solve a problem when you were upset, sad, angry, etc.? If so, what kind of effect do you think your emotions had on your ability to make the decision?

2. What do you think would make the decision-making process more effective?

To the Leader

If students are aware that the decision-making process can be influenced by emotions, they may be better able to set those emotions aside and make decisions based on their values and their consideration of alternatives and consequences.

Problems and Peer Pressure

Objective

To evaluate the impact of peer pressure on personal problem solving

Materials

Problems and Peer Pressure Worksheets (Handout 8)

Procedure

1. Distribute one Problems and Peer Pressure Worksheet (Handout 8) to each student. Ask students to read each situation and decide what they would do if this were their problem.
2. Divide students into groups of five and assign one problem to each group to discuss. Assign a recorder for each group. While individuals are sharing their decisions and discussing what factors they considered in arriving at a conclusion, the recorder is to jot down the ideas involved in the decision-making process.
3. Have groups share some of the factors that contributed to their decisions.

Discussion

Content Questions

1. How much of an influence did peer acceptance or approval play in the decision-making process you used in these situations?
2. What factors other than peer acceptance or approval seemed significant?
3. How wise is it to make a decision based on peer acceptance or approval? What might the consequences be of doing this frequently?

Personalization Questions

1. Have you ever made a decision based on peer acceptance or approval? Were you pleased with the decision you made and the consequences of the decision?

To the Leader

It is important that students recognize the factors involved in making a decision and understand that peer influence often plays an important role in this process. Having students look at the consequences of deciding solely on peer pressure is critical in developing a sound approach to decision making.

HANDOUT 8

Problems and Peer Pressure Worksheet

Directions: Read each situation carefully and decide what you would do in each case.

1. You and a friend go to a movie and sit in the back row. Just before the movie starts, a ninth grader comes up and asks you if you want to leave and go drink some beer. You really don't want to go, but your friend says yes right away. What do you do? Stay at the movie or go with them to drink?

2. You have invited a few kids to spend the night. After your parents are in bed, two of the kids open a pack of cigarettes and start to smoke. You feel uncomfortable and don't know whether to let them go ahead, tell them to stop, or call your parents. What do you do?

3. One of your friends has just gotten into the shower after physical education class. A few kids come up with a pair of scissors and want you to find your friend's jeans so that they can cut a slit in the crotch. You don't think it's a nice thing to do, but the kids are bullies and you are a little afraid. What do you do?

4. One of your friends invites you to stay overnight, and your parents ask you to check to see if the person's mother or father will be at home. Your friend asks you to say yes, even though no one but you and your friend will be there. Your friend tells you several other kids are also invited over for a party. What do you do? Tell your parents the truth, or tell them what your friend wants you to?

5. One of your friends has been acting strangely, especially at lunchtime. She hasn't been eating much of anything, and you have seen her hide some of her food in her napkin so the lunchroom supervisors don't get on her for not eating anything. You have also been around her when she has eaten a whole lot of food and has then spent quite a bit of time in one of the restrooms. You are afraid that she has an eating disorder, but once when you hinted at it she begged you not to say anything and told you that it wasn't anything to worry about. You think the problem is getting worse. What do you do?

What Can You Control?

Objective

To recognize which factors in a given problem are or are not under one's control

Materials

What Can You Control Worksheets (Handout 9); pens or pencils as needed

Procedure

1. Introduce the activity by discussing the fact that, even though we would like to be able to control all aspects of a given problem situation, such control oftentimes is not possible. For example, if your parents are getting a divorce and you are having some problems as a result, you cannot control the fact that your parents are getting a divorce, but you can control your reaction to certain aspects of the problem and make decisions about the parts of the problem that affect you.

2. Distribute one copy of the What Can You Control Worksheet (Handout 9) to each student. Ask students to read each situation, mark the continuum according to the degree to which they feel they have control, and note exactly what they might be able to do in the situation.

3. When students are finished, share responses to the questions in the larger group.

Discussion

Content Questions

1. Were you able to control more aspects of the problem than you first thought you could?

2. Do you think there is any problem you can't control some aspects of, at least to some degree? Share examples.

3. Was it difficult for you to decide how much control you had in some situations? Which ones were most difficult?

Personalization Questions

1. Have you ever had a problem and realized that you could control some parts of it but not others? Share examples.

2. Do you feel better knowing that, even though you can't control everything about a problem, you can control some things?

3. What have you learned from this lesson that you can apply to your life?

To the Leader

Problem situations have multiple factors, some of which are generally under a person's control. For example, although a student may not be able to control the fact that an older sister has become pregnant, the student can be extra supportive of her, continue to accept her, etc.

What Can You Control Worksheet

Directions: Read each situation and place a mark on the continuum to indicate how much control you think you have over it. If you do have some control, write down what you think you can do about the problem.

1. You want a certain boy or girl to go with you to the dance on Saturday.

   No control at all _____ Total control

   What can you do?

2. Your mom lost her job, and your family is really strapped for money.

   No control at all _____ Total control

   What can you do?

3. You just found out that your older sister, a junior in high school, is pregnant.

   No control at all _____ Total control

   What can you do?

4. Someone in your class continually teases you, and you don't like it.

   No control at all _____ Total control

   What can you do?

5. You are failing a subject in school.

   No control at all _____ Total control

   What can you do?

6. Your best friend hates his or her parents and is threatening to run away from home.

   No control at all _____ Total control

   What can you do?

Delaying Solutions

Objective

To learn that some problems cannot be solved immediately and to develop skills for dealing with delays

Materials

Paper and pencils as needed

Procedure

1. Ask students to think about five problems they have had in the past 2 years and to write down a short description of each problem on a piece of paper. Indicate that what they write down will be confidential unless they choose to share it.

2. Write the following code on the board while students are completing their problem descriptions.

> SP = serious
>
> MP = mild
>
> LL = long lasting (more than a few hours)
>
> ST = short term (a few hours or less)
>
> SA = solved alone
>
> NH = needed help to solve

3. Explain the coding system and have students assign three codes to each of their problems. For example, fighting with a sibling might be a fairly mild problem (MP). However, it could also be long lasting (LL), and you might need help (NH) to solve it.

4. Invite students to share examples of their problems and codings if they wish.

Discussion

Content Questions

1. What did you discover when you coded your problems? Were they mostly serious or mild? Long lasting or short term? Easily solved or not?

2. What do you think is the difference between a serious problem, for which there may not be an immediate solution, and a less serious problem, which could have a more immediate solution?

Personalization Questions

1. When you have had a serious problem without an immediate solution, how have you coped until the problem was worked out?

2. What have you learned about problems and their solutions?

To the Leader

The discussion questions can help students see that understanding the basic nature of a problem can be helpful in reaching a solution. Students may come up with other useful techniques, such as positive self-talk, getting busy doing other things and not dwelling on the problem, not expecting a perfect solution, etc.

Imaging the Solution

Objective

To learn the value of imagery as a problem-solving technique

Materials

None

Procedure

1. Introduce the lesson by asking students to recall a time when they first learned to do something, such as ride a bike, waterski, skate, etc. Discuss how they think they were able to learn this particular skill.

2. Next ask students to imagine that they are going to learn to walk a tightrope. Discuss the steps that might be necessary in learning to do this, such as first being able to balance oneself on the rope, then taking steps across the rope, obtaining the correct position of hands and feet, knowing how to get off the rope, etc. Invite them to close their eyes and visualize themselves slowly walking up the ladder, gently stepping onto the rope, balancing with both arms, putting one foot in front of the other, etc.

3. After discussing this sequence, invite students to think of problems they have had recently that involved taking a risk, telling someone something, doing something they were afraid to do, etc. Encourage them to use imaging to visualize one step of the problem at a time. Share experiences.

Discussion

Content Questions

1. Were you able to image a solution or the steps to a resolution of the problem situation?
2. Do you think a procedure like this is useful? If so, why?

Personalization Questions

1. Have you ever tried to use imaging in order to see solutions to problems? If so, what types of problems were they, and how did the technique work for you? (Invite students to share examples, such as those occurring in sports, where imaging is often used.)
2. Is imaging something you will use to help break a problem into manageable parts?

To the Leader

Imaging is often a good way of moderating strong feelings when faced with a seemingly insurmountable problem.

Looking Long Term

Objective

To develop the ability to identify short-term goals in order to achieve long-term goals

Materials

Separate index cards, on which are written the following: *President of the United States, president of a company, teacher, politician, movie star,* etc.

Procedure

1. Discuss what the word *goal* means (an end toward which one strives). Indicate that some goals are short term in that they can be accomplished quickly. Other goals are long term and may take years to accomplish. In order for long-term goals to be realized, a series of short-term goals leading to the end result must be established.

2. Divide students into groups of four and give each group one of the previously prepared index cards. The group's task is to identify the short-term goals the person noted on the card might have established in order to achieve his or her long-term goal.

3. After allowing a few minutes to brainstorm goals, have each group share several examples. Emphasize the fact that long-term goals aren't achieved overnight, but that successful people have been able to identify a series of short-term goals leading up to what they ultimately want to accomplish.

4. Invite students to share examples of some of their own personal goals.

Discussion

Content Questions

1. What is the difference between long- and short-term goals?
2. How do you think people decide on long-term goals?
3. How were you able to identify the short-term goals for this activity?

Personalization Questions

1. Do you have any long-term goals? If you do, how do you think having them will help you in the future? Share examples.
2. Have you identified any short-term goals that will help you achieve your long-term goals? Share examples.

To the Leader

Helping students see that long-term goals must be preceded by a progression of short-term goals may also help them realize that nothing meaningful can be accomplished without continued effort.

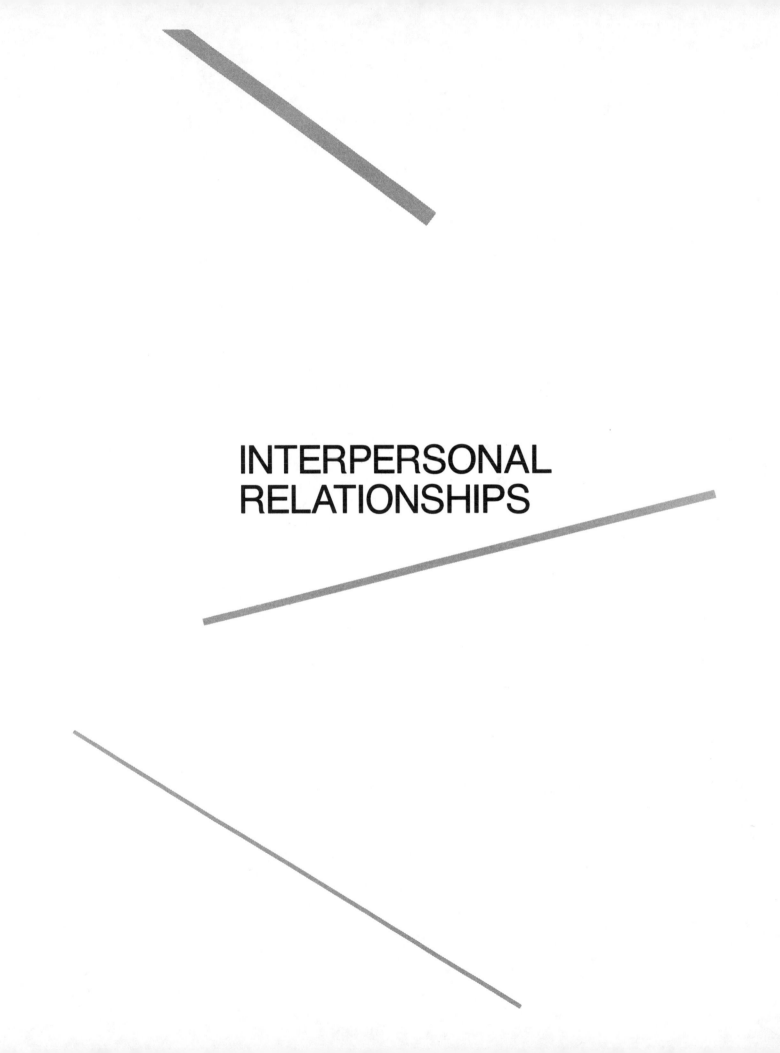

INTERPERSONAL
RELATIONSHIPS

Should They or Shouldn't They?

Objective

To learn to distinguish between reasonable and unreasonable *shoulds* for others

Materials

One set of Should They or Shouldn't They Statements and a Sorting Board for each pair of students

Procedure

1. Introduce the activity by asking students to respond to the following statements by raising a hand high if they strongly agree, keeping it level if they agree somewhat, and putting it down if they disagree strongly.

    Teachers should never give low grades.

    Parents should always let their kids do anything they want to do.

    Kids should never have to do chores around the house.

    A friend should always stand by you no matter what.

2. Discuss responses, directing particular attention to the absolutistic nature of the statements: Is it realistic for kids *never* to have chores to do? Is it reasonable for parents to let their kids do *whatever* they want to do?

3. Distribute one set of Should They or Shouldn't They Statements and a Sorting Board to each pair of students. Have pairs sort the statements into piles according to the categories listed on the board.

Discussion

Content Questions

1. Which category had the most shoulds: *reasonable, unreasonable,* or *depends?*

2. What do you think is the difference between these categories of shoulds? In other words, what makes something unreasonable or reasonable? What has to be considered as you decide what is reasonable or unreasonable?

3. Which type of should do you think is most frequent in relationships with parents? Teachers? Friends?

Personalization Questions

1. Do you think you have a greater number of reasonable or unreasonable shoulds for others? With which group do you find yourself being most unreasonable? Most reasonable?

2. How do you think your shoulds affect your relationships with your peers, parents, or teachers?

3. What are some other examples of shoulds that you have for others? Are these reasonable or unreasonable? Share examples.

4. How can you apply what you have learned to your relationships with others?

To the Leader

Relationships will likely be affected adversely if an abundance of unreasonable shoulds exist. It is very important to challenge students to think about such demands and to sort out what is truly reasonable to expect in a relationship.

Should They or Shouldn't They Statements

Directions: Copy each statement on a separate slip of paper or index card.

Parents

Parents should let their kids hang out with anyone they want.

Parents should provide their kids with food and shelter.

Parents should listen to their kids.

Parents should never ask questions about what their kids are doing.

If parents drink alcohol, they should let their kids drink it too.

Teachers

Teachers should always give good grades.

Teachers should try to be fair.

Teachers should not call students names.

Teachers should not allow kids to cheat.

Teachers should always have exciting, stimulating classes.

Peers

A good friend should always stand up for you, even if it means he or she might get in trouble.

A good friend should agree with everything you do.

A good friend should never let you down.

A good friend should believe the same way you do about things.

A good friend shouldn't hang around with other kids as much as with you.

Sorting Board

Directions: Make one board for each pair of students, using posterboard or other heavy paper.

	Reasonable	Unreasonable	Depends
Parents			
Teachers			
Peers			

How Irritating?

Objective

To learn to differentiate between irritating, unpleasant, and intolerable situations in interpersonal relationships

Materials

How Irritating Worksheets (Handout 10); pens or pencils as needed

Procedure

1. Discuss the meaning of the words *irritating, unpleasant,* and *intolerable,* emphasizing that there is a difference in degree in these terms similar to the degrees on a thermometer. In other words, if something upsets you a little bit, it is irritating, but if something is very offensive, it might be considered intolerable.

2. Discuss how understanding these terms could apply to relationships with others by using the following example.

   A friend asks to borrow one of your sweaters, saying that he or she will return it the next day. When your friend doesn't return the sweater, you might be irritated. But suppose two or three days go by, the sweater hasn't been returned, and your parent is asking where it is. The situation might now be unpleasant. Then suppose this friend started telling everyone the sweater actually was his or hers. You might think this situation was intolerable.

3. Divide students in to groups of three and distribute a How Irritating Worksheet (Handout 10) to each group. Designate one person to record the group's responses on the worksheet. Groups are first to think about things they find irritating in relationships with others. (They are not to use names but are to give general examples, such as having someone forget to call at a certain time.) Next ask groups to think of examples of things that are unpleasant in relationships. (An example might be having someone ask you to do something that would force you to lie about where you were going.) Finally, ask for examples of things the groups might find intolerable. (An example might be having one of your relatives get arrested for murdering someone.)

4. Start with the situations identified as irritating and have groups share some examples, recording them on the chalkboard. Have them next share examples of unpleasant and then intolerable situations. Once lists of all three types are on the board, discuss the groups' responses, using the Content and Personalization Questions.

Discussion

Content Questions

1. Were examples of what was irritating, unpleasant, or intolerable to one group necessarily the same as those that were irritating, unpleasant, or intolerable to another group? What do you suppose accounts for this difference? (Reiterate the fact that our degree of discomfort is related to what we *think* about a particular event.)

Personalization Questions

1. How did your group decide what examples should go in the different categories? In other words, what distinguishes an irritation from something intolerable? (Help students clarify this idea by pointing out the influence of their beliefs about right and wrong, what and who is important, etc.)

2. How do these degrees of discomfort affect your relationships with other people? What are some of the behaviors you exhibit or some feelings you have when something is irritating, unpleasant, or intolerable?

To the Leader

Students will likely give a wide range of responses in deciding what is irritating, unpleasant, or intolerable. Be sure to tease out these differences and emphasize that they occur because our beliefs and values differ. (Have students save the worksheet from this lesson for the next activity.)

How Irritating Worksheet

Directions: List each of the relationship problems brainstormed by the group in the most appropriate category.

Irritating	Unpleasant	Intolerable

The Conflict-Belief Connection

Objective

To recognize the connection between interpersonal conflict and irrational beliefs and to learn how to challenge such beliefs in order to improve relationships

Materials

How Irritating Worksheets (Handout 10 from Grades 7–8 Interpersonal Relationships Activity 2); paper and pencils as needed

Procedure

1. Review the discussion from Grades 7–8 Interpersonal Relationships Activity 2 (How Irritating?), stressing the importance of beliefs in determining what one considers to be irritating, unpleasant, or intolerable in relationships with others. For instance, if you get asked to a dance, it could be irritating if you don't particularly like the person, unpleasant if you don't like the person at all, and intolerable if you don't approve of the person's reputation or have had previous negative experiences with the person. The key is the *beliefs* you have about the person or situation involving that person.

2. Take several examples from the lists generated in the previous activity and, as a class, elicit the beliefs that resulted in the situation's being designated irritating, unpleasant, or intolerable. Use the following model in discussing the idea.

   > There's a big party this weekend, and you haven't been invited. The situation might be irritating if you don't particularly like parties, don't care about the people who are going, and have something else to do anyway. It might be unpleasant if you really think you should have been invited, believe no one likes you because you weren't invited, or assume you will have a miserable time because you can't go. It might seem intolerable if you think you'll never get invited to another party or that nothing will ever be the same again.

3. Using the student-generated examples, discuss what happens between people when beliefs begin to interfere. In some cases (usually when the situation is only irritating), the relationship isn't affected much, but in other cases it could be. For instance, if you found it intolerable and absolutely unacceptable and awful that someone didn't call you at the time you expected, you would probably be angry, and your anger would in turn affect the way you interacted with the person.

4. Next ask students to think of an example of a conflict they have had recently with another person. Instruct them to write down a brief description of this conflict.

5. Introduce the idea of thinking through and challenging the beliefs you have about the person or situation in conflict. For example, if someone didn't call at the time you expected, it could be that the person doesn't care, but it could also be that something else came up. Is it actually the end of the world? Is it something worth getting really upset about? Encourage students to ask themselves questions to clarify the situation. Have students take some of the examples and generate a list of challenges for each one.

Discussion

Content Questions

1. What is the connection between beliefs and degree of discomfort (irritating, unpleasant, intolerable)?
2. What happens to relationships as a result of our beliefs?
3. What effect does challenging have on relationships?

Personalization Questions

1. How have your relationships with others been affected by your beliefs?
2. Have you ever tried to challenge your beliefs or rethink things? Did doing this change the degree to which you felt discomfort?

To the Leader

The more irrational beliefs are challenged, the greater the chance people will feel irritated instead of having stronger feelings about interpersonal relationships. Because our thoughts influence the degree of positive or negative feelings in relationships, the skill of challenging is particularly important. Unless the thoughts behind the conflict are resolved, the conflict will not be resolved.

Approval and Consequences

Objective

To recognize the advantages and disadvantages of doing something to gain social approval

Materials

Approval and Consequences Worksheets (Handout 11); magazine pictures of people drinking beer, kissing, fighting, smoking, etc.

Procedure

1. Hold up the magazine pictures and ask students to describe what they see happening. Indicate that sometimes people do these things because they want to, but other times they do them because they want to be accepted by others. Ask students to pair up and think of other examples of things that could be done to get others' approval (taking drugs, making out, getting caught up in fad diets or clothing fads, etc.). List examples on the chalkboard.

2. Discuss the difference between doing something because you feel it is right for you and doing something that doesn't feel right but that you do because the crowd is doing it and you want their approval. Discuss the concept of consequences of doing things for peer approval, using the following example.

   Tony is a good student, but the kids he runs around with think doing your homework and being smart means that you are a nerd. So Tony stops studying and gets bad grades so he'll fit in.

3. Distribute one Approval and Consequences Worksheet (Handout 11) per pair and have students complete the exercise. (Students should save these worksheets for the next activity.)

4. Discuss responses.

Discussion

Content Questions

1. What are some of the consequences that have to be considered when deciding whether or not to do something?

2. What happens if you go against the crowd and do what you think is right for you?

Personalization Questions

1. When you are confronted with a conflict of this type, what process do you go through in deciding what to do?

2. If you go with the crowd but against what you think might be right for you, how do you feel?

3. Have you learned anything from this activity that you could apply to future conflict situations involving peer approval?

To the Leader

Many times, in wanting peer approval, young people don't carefully assess the consequences of their actions. Because serious consequences can result from drinking, taking drugs, engaging in premarital sex, etc., it is vital that students look at the consequences of giving in to peer pressure. (Have students save the worksheet from this lesson for the next activity.)

HANDOUT 11

Approval and Consequences Worksheet

Directions: Read each situation, then list the consequences if you did or didn't give in to peer pressure.

1. Chad and Tom are going to a movie. Next to the theater is a video arcade. Because they have a few minutes before the movie starts, they go inside. They see some kids from their school who invite them to come out in the parking lot and have a few beers. What could happen if Chad and Tom go? What could happen if they don't go?

2. Marcia and Tim have been going out for about a month. Tim calls Marcia and tells her that his parents are gone for the night and he wants her to come over. Tim is older and has been urging Marcia not to be so uptight about making out with him. Marcia really likes Tim but can't decide what to do. What could happen if Marcia does go? What could happen if she doesn't go?

3. Jenny and Sarah have been friends for a long time, but lately Jenny has been hanging around with a different crowd and hasn't called Sarah much. However, Jenny calls and asks Sarah to a party Friday night. Sarah goes to the party, but when she gets there, she notices that lots of kids are smoking pot. Jenny urges Sarah to try it, saying that it won't hurt anything. What could happen if Sarah does try it? What could happen if she doesn't try it?

4. Tonya is really smart, but she gets tired of having her friends call her a nerd and a bookworm all the time. Since she's been little, she has wanted to be a doctor. When her friends call and want her to do things and she says she has to study, they make fun of her. She thinks she might be losing her friends. What could happen if Tonya continues to study? What could happen if she doesn't continue to study?

5. Think of your own situation!

Stand Up for Yourself!

Objective

To learn assertion skills in response to peer pressure

Materials

Approval and Consequences Worksheets (Handout 11 from Grades 7–8 Interpersonal Relationships Activity 4)

Procedure

1. Discuss some of the consequences students identified in Grades 7–8 Interpersonal Relationships Activity 4 (Approval and Consequences). Introduce the concept of nonassertive and assertive behavior as ways of dealing with peer pressure. Nonassertion means that you would probably go along with what your peers suggest, even though you don't feel comfortable and know that the consequences might be serious. Assertion means that you recognize what is best for you and are able to stand up for what you believe in, but not in an obnoxious manner.

2. Use one of the examples from Activity 4 and ask for volunteers to role play the peers in the situation. Demonstrate nonassertive and then assertive responses.

   For example: Chad and Tom are going to a movie. Next to the theater is a video arcade. Because they have a few minutes before the movie starts, they go inside. They see some kids from their school who invite them to come out in the parking lot and have a few beers.

   Nonassertive response: Chad and Tom don't really want to go but are afraid to say no, so they stay and drink.

   Assertive response: Chad and Tom say they'd rather not and walk away.

3. Divide students into groups of five and have them role play the rest of the example situations. Debrief by discussing the Content and Personalization Questions.

Discussion

Content Questions

1. What do you see as the difference between assertive and nonassertive behavior? What are the payoffs for each?

2. Are there some situations in which it is more difficult than others to be assertive? Explain.

Personalization Questions

1. Have you ever been assertive or nonassertive in relationships with others? Share examples.

2. Which type of behavior works best for you? Which type will better help you do what is in your own best interests?

To the Leader

Many good resources exist for teaching assertive behavior. See especially *The Assertive Option: Your Rights and Responsibilities*, by P. Jakubowski and A.J. Lange, 1978, Champaign, IL: Research Press.

Accepting Others

Objective

To learn to accept others for who they are rather than who we think they should be

Materials

Paper and pencils as needed

Procedure

1. Read the following scenario aloud.

   > Kathy is upset with her best friend because her friend always has her hair hanging in her eyes and is pushing it back and running her fingers through it. She's also always late—if she says she'll be there in 10 minutes, it's always longer. Kathy also hates it that her friend's room is so messy. Her friend can never find anything, so she always wants to borrow things from Kathy. Usually Kathy tries not to let this stuff bother her, but it bugs her that her friend can't be more like her.

2. Discuss the scenario. Does Kathy have a right to get upset about these things? Can Kathy do anything about them? Are they things that are worth getting upset about?

3. Have students think about a person whose behavior bugs them. Have them list some of the things that person does without identifying the person.

4. Encourage students to share some examples of things that bug them in their relationships with others.

Discussion

Content Questions

1. Do you think the things that bug you about others are things that are important enough to get upset about?

2. Do you think you can do anything to change these things? Are there some things you should try to change? How do you go about deciding which things are worth trying to change?

3. Do you think it is reasonable to expect that others will always act as you want them to? If not, what do you need to do so you will be able to get along better with them?

Personalization Questions

1. In your relationships, how much right do you think you have to tell others how to act?

2. If you have been in a situation like the one described, what exactly did you think you did or didn't have a right to be bothered about?

To the Leader

It is easy to allow ourselves to get bothered about little things that others do. Emphasize that you can't change other people, only your reaction to them. Since we do have a choice in such matters, it is also good to help students determine what is really worth getting upset about.

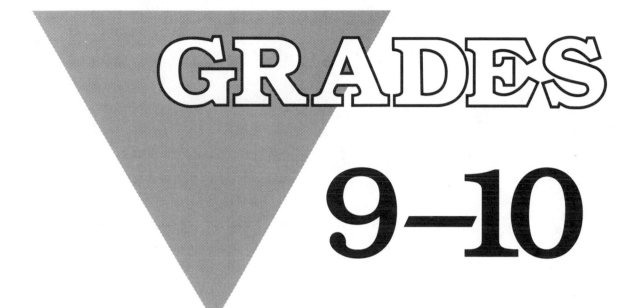

GRADES
9–10

SELF-ACCEPTANCE

Erase the Slate

Objective

To recognize that past behavior doesn't have to influence present self-concept

Materials

Paper and pencils as needed

Procedure

1. Introduce the lesson by discussing how behaving in shameful ways in the past might influence us in the present. Share a personal example of something you did as a child, adolescent, or adult that you felt ashamed about.

2. Stressing confidentiality, invite students to jot down one or more situations they consider shameful in their own lives. Emphasize that we all experience situations of this nature, but that what is shameful to one person isn't necessarily so to another.

3. Ask students if they know of people (perhaps famous movie stars or athletes) who have done something that might have been considered shameful, such as getting involved in drugs or in trouble with the police. Discuss the effects of such behavior on these people's lives. Did they overcome the problem and turn their lives around, or did they continue on the same track?

Discussion

Content Questions

1. Do you think you have to feel ashamed forever about something you did in the past?
2. What good does it do to hang on to shameful feelings?
3. Do you think that even if you have had some pretty bad experiences you can turn your life around?

Personalization Questions

1. What's one thing you have done or can do to erase the effects of past behavior about which you felt ashamed?
2. What does it say about you if you have had some shameful experiences in the past?

To the Leader

It is important for students to realize that their past behavior doesn't have to influence them in the present. If they have done things they consider shameful, they can learn from those experiences and go on with life. Stress that everyone makes mistakes and that what people do isn't who they are.

What's Important to Me

Objective

To clarify personal values

Materials

Paper and pencils as needed

Procedure

1. Ask students to share something they value. Explain that a value is chosen freely (no one else makes you value it), prized (you feel good about having the value), and acted upon (your behavior is consistent with what you say about the value). For example, if a person values freedom, he or she would be willing to march publicly for freedom of an oppressed group and would feel right about doing it.

2. Invite students to write down 5–10 things they value. These could include beliefs, possessions, behaviors, etc.

3. Next ask students to put a *C* beside each value they think they have freely chosen. If they prize this value, they should put a *P* next to it. If they act upon the value, they should label it with an *A*. (Point out that acting on a value may mean taking direct action, such as marching or contributing money, but it may also mean speaking up and owning the fact that this is something you value.)

Discussion

Content Questions

1. Do most of the items on your list include the three criteria (chosen, prized, and acted upon)?

2. Was it difficult to think of things you value?

Personalization Questions

1. What did you learn about your values from this activity?

2. If you discovered that you don't act on your values, what can you do about it?

3. What can you do if you don't value something others do? Should you change your mind even if it would be hard for you to prize the value?

4. Have your values changed in the past few years? How? Do you think they will continue to change?

To the Leader

Help students think about acting in a way consistent with what they say they believe, distinguish what they value from what others value, and understand that, if we don't feel right about doing something, it is not something we value.

Criticism

Objective

To differentiate criticism of what one does from criticism of who one is

Materials

Paper and pencils as needed

Procedure

1. Introduce the activity by asking for a volunteer to define what the word *criticism* means (the act of finding fault, disapproving, or making critical judgment).

2. Ask students to identify quickly in writing a time when they have been criticized. They are to describe this time by answering the following questions.

> What was the situation?
>
> Where did the situation take place?
>
> When did the situation occur?
>
> Who was involved?
>
> How did you feel in the situation?

3. Invite students to share their examples in groups of three.

Discussion

Content Questions

1. What was it like to recall a situation in which you were criticized?
2. Did you find that anyone else had a situation similar to yours?
3. How did the people in your group generally feel about being criticized?

Personalization Questions

1. Just because someone criticizes you, does this mean you're no good? Does it mean you have done something wrong? What does it mean?
2. What is it like for you to get criticism? How do you feel, and what do you say to yourself? Share examples.
3. Do you think it is natural to be criticized sometimes?

To the Leader

Stress that criticism is natural and unavoidable, but that it does not reflect on a person's intrinsic worth.

You're Great!

Objective

To learn to accept compliments

Materials

None

Procedure

1. Ask for a volunteer to define the word *compliment* (a statement made in admiration or praise). Ask students to brainstorm examples of compliments they have received and write their examples on the chalkboard.

2. Next ask students to describe how they feel about getting compliments (happy, embarrassed, etc.). Also ask them how they feel and act when they give them.

3. Divide students into pairs. Partner 1 gives Partner 2 a compliment, either an original one or one from the examples already generated. Partner 2 is to accept the compliment and then discuss how he or she felt getting it. Have students switch partners and repeat the process.

Discussion

Content Questions

1. How did you feel when you were being complimented? How different was this role-play situation from being complimented in real life?

Personalization Questions

1. When you receive a compliment, what do you think this says about you?

2. If you are not comfortable receiving compliments, what can you do about it?

3. Are you a person who tends to give a lot of compliments? Do you give them more often to persons of your own sex or persons of the opposite sex? How do you feel about giving compliments?

To the Leader

Helping students accept compliments without feeling apologetic or embarrassed will help them develop greater self-acceptance.

Success/Failure

Objective

To distinguish between succeeding or failing at something and being a success or failure as a person

Materials

Paper and pencils as needed

Procedure

1. Divide students into small groups (5–6 members) and write the word *success* on the chalkboard. Ask students to share for 10 minutes their ideas of what success means to them. Ask one student per group to be a recorder and write down responses.
2. Ask each recorder to summarize his or her group's definition of success. Write these definitions on the board.
3. Next write the word *failure* on the board and have groups discuss what failure means to them. Have the recorder take notes and report as before.
4. Write the groups' definitions on the board.

Discussion

Content Questions

1. How similar or different were definitions within the groups?
2. Why do you think definitions of success and failure differ from person to person?

Personalization Questions

1. Do you think succeeding or failing at something means that you have succeeded or failed as a person?
2. What does it mean to you to succeed or fail?

To the Leader

The distinction between succeeding or failing at something but not as a person is very important. It is likewise necessary for students to understand that definitions of success and failure depend on individual perceptions rather than on universal definitions.

Increase Your Successes

Objective

To develop goal-setting techniques to overcome failures

Materials

Paper and pencils as needed

Procedure

1. Review the objective from Grades 9–10 Self-Awareness Activity 5 (Success/Failure), emphasizing that succeeding or failing at something doesn't mean that you as a person are a success or a failure. Ask students who has control over success and failure (you as an individual, someone else, or a circumstance). Share ideas to illustrate the issue of control.

2. Ask students to identify a situation in which they have not succeeded, such as not running as fast as they'd like to in a race, not dating as many people as they would like, not doing as well in a subject as they would prefer.

3. Introduce the concept of setting goals to overcome failures. Point out that a useful goal must be specific, doable, and realistic. For example, if you can't swim at all, it is not realistic to set your goal to be a champion swimmer in 2 months, but it is possible to call the recreation center, determine when swimming lessons begin, and sign up. If necessary, share some other examples of specific goals.

4. Have each student write down a useful goal for the situation previously identified.

Discussion

Content Questions

1. How difficult was it to set a goal for something in which you wanted to succeed? (Students can share examples in the group as a whole or in smaller groups, if desired.)

2. Just because you haven't been successful at something in the past, does that mean you can't be successful in the future?

3. Can you think of situations in which, no matter how many goals you set, you still wouldn't be able to attain success?

Personalization Questions

1. What can you do to increase your chances of success and minimize failure? How does specific goal setting relate to this concept?

To the Leader

It is important to help students set realistic goals and see that they have more control over events than they may think.

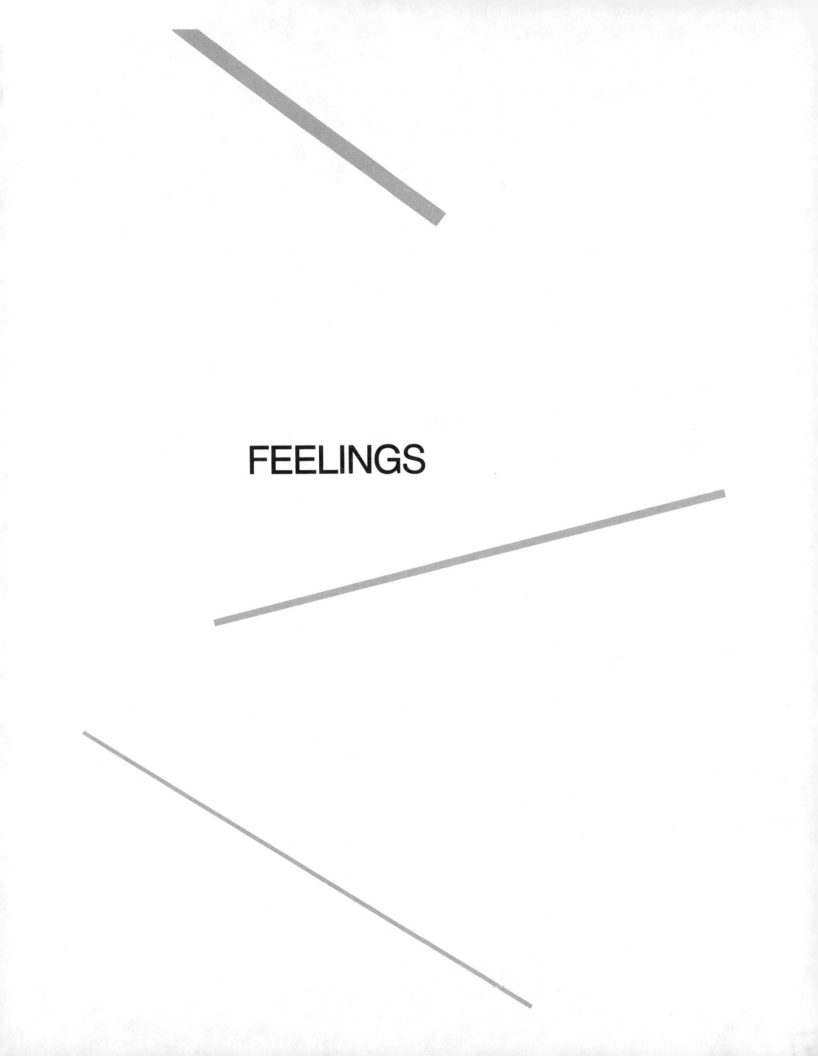

FEELINGS

Payoffs

Objective

To analyze the payoffs of pleasant versus unpleasant feelings

Materials

Payoffs Worksheets (Handout 12)

Procedure

1. Discuss what a payoff is (some kind of benefit that occurs due to a particular incident). For every situation, there are positive and negative payoffs. For example, if you were invited to a dance, the positive payoff could be having fun and meeting new kids. The negative payoff might be taking a risk—maybe you don't dance as well as some other kids and someone might laugh. Point out that it is important to learn to evaluate these payoffs so that we have a better understanding of feelings and behavior.

2. Explain that positive and negative payoffs are also associated with feelings. Sometimes people think there are no positive payoffs for negative feelings, but this is not the case. For example, if a person is feeling depressed, he or she might get a lot of attention, and this attention might even keep the person from shaking the depression.

3. Distribute the Payoffs Worksheets (Handout 12) and have students choose partners. Pairs are to identify what they think would be the positive and negative payoffs for the feelings listed.

4. Share responses in the larger group.

Discussion

Content Questions

1. Was it difficult to think of payoffs for feelings? Were some more difficult than others?

2. Why do you think it is important to analyze payoffs?

Personalization Questions

1. Have you ever held onto a feeling even though the payoffs weren't helping you? Why might you have done this?

2. Next time you experience a feeling and find that the payoffs for having that feeling are not all that great, what can you do about it?

To the Leader

Students need to recognize that we all occasionally hold onto negative feelings for the wrong reasons. Having a choice and knowing how to analyze the payoffs for feelings is helpful in taking charge of the situation.

Payoffs Worksheet

Directions: Identify a positive and negative payoff for having the following feelings.

1. Angry

   Positive:

   Negative:

2. Depressed

   Positive:

   Negative:

3. Sad

   Positive:

   Negative:

4. Happy

   Positive:

   Negative:

5. Confused

   Positive:

   Negative:

6. Lonely

   Positive:

   Negative:

Reactions

Objective

To distinguish between reasonable and unreasonable reactions to emotions

Materials

Paper and pencils as needed

Procedure

1. Discuss the concept of reacting to emotions. For instance, if you feel depressed, you might stay in bed all day, not smile, withdraw from friends, or even use drugs. If you are angry, you might throw things, get drunk, drive too fast, or keep your anger bottled up inside.

2. With students, generate a list of common feeling words and write them on the chalkboard. Then have students form groups of four and assign each group four of the identified feelings. Groups then brainstorm all of the ways someone with those feelings might react.

3. Share examples of reactions and record responses on the board.

4. Next discuss the idea that some reactions are more reasonable than others. Unreasonable reactions might, for example, be out of proportion to the event, might hurt someone, or might damage something. Ask students to go through their lists for each feeling and put a plus sign beside those reactions they see as reasonable and a minus sign beside those they see as unreasonable.

5. Share ratings in the larger group.

Discussion

Content Questions

1. Was it difficult to think of emotional reactions?
2. Which reactions were more easily identified—reasonable or unreasonable?
3. What is the difference between reasonable and unreasonable reactions?

Personalization Questions

1. Which type of reaction is most characteristic of you?
2. Which type of expression do you think is healthier? What can you do to increase this type of expression?

To the Leader

Emotional expression is a choice, and it is important for students to identify those reactions that are positive and in their own best interests.

Moods

Objective

To identify various moods and to develop strategies for dealing with moodiness

Materials

None

Procedure

1. Define the words *mood* and *moody*. (A mood is a particular state of mind or feeling; being moody is to feel gloomy or sullen or to have changes of mood.)

2. Ask students how many of them have ever been moody. Ask for some examples of different types of moods they experience. Also discuss mood swings, in which you may be up one day, down the next (or experience changes in feelings even more rapidly than this). Emphasize that feeling moody and having mood swings are natural, but that if moodiness begins to be a problem it is good to talk to a counselor or a parent.

3. Discuss what students do when they experience moods or mood swings. How does this affect behavior? Emphasize the connection between moods and behaviors and elicit some examples of what the effects of moodiness are (changes in eating or drinking habits, being "short" with people, overreacting to minor events, etc.).

Discussion

Content Questions

1. Do you think there are any payoffs for being moody?

2. What are some things that can be done to deal with moodiness?

Personalization Questions

1. Would you characterize yourself as a moody person?

2. What's your experience being around others who are moody? Do you enjoy their company? What do you usually do about others' moods, if anything?

3. What do you think you can do to deal with your moodiness next time it occurs?

To the Leader

At this age, moods and mood swings are natural, but it is helpful for students to realize that they don't always have to be the victims of their moods. They can exercise control by going out with others or engaging in activities even if they don't feel like doing so, setting useful goals, talking out feelings, etc.

Guilt and Shame

Objective

To identify ways to deal with guilt and shame

Materials

Paper and pencils as needed

Procedure

1. Write the definition of the word *guilt* on the chalkboard (a painful feeling of self-reproach resulting from a belief that one has done something wrong or immoral). Discuss the definition.

2. Write the definition of the word *shame* on the board (a feeling of having lost respect because of improper behavior or incompetence). Discuss.

3. Ask students to write a short paragraph describing something about which they have felt guilty or ashamed. Indicate that what they write will be confidential unless they care to share it.

4. Take an example of something that students this age might feel guilty about, such as lying to parents about where they have been or telling a friend they were busy when they really wanted to do something else. Ask students to raise their hands if they would feel guilty about this situation. Assuming that some will and some won't, elicit reasons for this, stressing the concept of self-talk. For example, some of the self-talk messages a person might send after lying to a friend might be "I should have been honest and told the truth," "I should have gone even if I didn't want to," and "Because I lied, maybe I hurt this person's feelings."

5. Have students think of other examples and point out that, when we feel guilty about something, we often subsequently feel ashamed. Shame can also occur without guilt, such as feeling shame over the fact that your parents drink too much, because you aren't as competent as you'd like to be, or because someone in your family has done something to give the family a bad reputation.

6. Discuss the fact that we may do things we feel guilty about because we are afraid to take a risk and say no or tell the truth. For example, if you told your parents where you had been instead of lying, they might get mad and ground you—or they might not get that mad. Sometimes we assume the worst will happen when, in reality, it doesn't.

7. Have students share examples of the self-talk involved in situations in which they have felt guilty. Emphasize the importance of thinking through how valid the assumptions about the situation really are. Shame also occurs because we assume that people will think terrible things about us if we expose ourselves. Frequently, if we are able to be open about ourselves or our experiences, we find others have had similar experiences. This in turn can help us feel less ashamed.

Discussion

Content Questions

1. Do you think guilt and shame are healthy emotions?
2. Do you think people enjoy feeling guilty or ashamed?
3. Do you think there is any way to prevent people from feeling guilty or ashamed?

Personalization Questions

1. Do you enjoy feeling guilty or ashamed? Do these feelings do you any good?
2. If you have ever felt guilty or ashamed, have you tried anything to keep those feelings from being so powerful?

To the Leader

Guilt and shame are natural but often unnecessary if we are willing to be open. Positive self-talk can also help to reduce put-downs and awfulizing, which can make guilt and shame worse.

Worry, Fear, and Anxiety

Objective

To identify ways to deal with worry, fear, and anxiety

Materials

Worry, Fear, and Anxiety Surveys (Handout 13)

Procedure

1. Ask for a show of hands indicating how many students have ever been worried, afraid, or anxious about anything. Assure them that these feelings are normal, but explain that it is also good to find ways to deal with them.

2. Distribute one Worry, Fear, and Anxiety Survey (Handout 13) per student. Inform students that all responses will remain confidential unless they wish to share them.

3. Divide students into groups of 3–4 and have them select a recorder, whose task is to write down all suggestions the group brainstorms for dealing with worry, fear, and anxiety. At this time, students may also share any specific concerns from the survey and ask the group for ideas on how to deal with particular issues.

4. Invite each group to share solutions for dealing with these emotions.

Discussion

Content Questions

1. Were you surprised at the ratings you gave the various items on the survey? What does this indicate to you?

2. Do you think it is natural for people to experience these emotions? Is there a point at which these feelings become unhealthy?

Personalization Questions

1. Which of the strategies for dealing with these emotions have you tried? How did they work for you?

2. What are some strategies you would like to try?

To the Leader

Stress that, although everyone experiences these emotions to varying degrees, strategies exist for dealing with them. Through discussion, help students identify such things as talking out worries with friends or adults, being assertive, reading pertinent self-help books or articles, setting goals, or seeing a counselor.

HANDOUT 13

Worry, Fear, and Anxiety Survey

Directions: Put a checkmark next to each item to show how much you worry about, fear, or are anxious about it.

	Frequently	Sometimes	Never
Parents' fighting	☐	☐	☐
Money	☐	☐	☐
Parents' drinking	☐	☐	☐
Peer pressure	☐	☐	☐
Grades	☐	☐	☐
My future	☐	☐	☐
Dating	☐	☐	☐
How I look	☐	☐	☐
Sex	☐	☐	☐
Drugs	☐	☐	☐
Nuclear war	☐	☐	☐
Jobs	☐	☐	☐
Others' opinions	☐	☐	☐
Not being popular	☐	☐	☐
Performances	☐	☐	☐
What I say	☐	☐	☐
Weight	☐	☐	☐
Athletics	☐	☐	☐
Acceptance	☐	☐	☐
AIDS	☐	☐	☐
Getting sick	☐	☐	☐
Growing up	☐	☐	☐

Tough Emotions

Objective

To develop the ability to modify intense negative feelings

Materials

Tough Emotions Worksheets (Handout 14)

Procedure

1. Ask students how many of them would like to eliminate or modify intensely negative feelings, such as being very angry or feeling extremely upset or anxious. Invite them to share examples of ways in which they have tried to achieve this.

2. Distribute one Tough Emotions Worksheet (Handout 14) per student and explain that it illustrates an alternative that can be used when students feel intensely negative.

3. Ask someone to share an event that resulted in an intense feeling. Following the pattern illustrated in the example given, write this event on the chalkboard in the A column. Next identify the feelings and behavioral consequences of the event; write these in the C column. Then elicit the irrational beliefs that contributed to the person's feelings; list them in the B column. (Point out that, when intense feelings exist, the accompanying beliefs aren't usually very sensible. These beliefs may be exaggerations, self put-downs, awfulizing, demands, etc.)

4. Show students how they can ask themselves disputing or challenging questions (column D) to "poke holes" in their faulty thinking. These questions make beliefs more sensible and can result in a new effect (column E). Doing so doesn't mean that the feeling will be wonderful, but it can be less intense and less negative.

5. Have students think of a personal example and complete the process on their own worksheets.

Discussion

Content Questions

1. Do you think this strategy can work in deintensifying negative feelings?
2. What do you think might be the most difficult part about making this system work?

Personalization Questions

1. Have you ever used this system for dealing with negative feelings? If so, how did it work for you?
2. How can you apply this information to personal situations?

To the Leader

Demonstrating the A–B–C–D–E method is a good way to teach emotional control. It may be necessary to go over these ideas several times so that students clearly understand conc~ (in particular, the concept of challenging).

Example Tough Emotions Worksheet Responses

A	B	C	D	E
Event	Irrational Beliefs	Emotional and Behavioral Consequences	Disputing or Challenging Questions	New Effects
Got grounded for a week.	1. It's not fair . . . I shouldn't be grounded. 2. I can't stand being grounded. It's awful! I'll just die.	Angry—threw phone across the room.	1. I can understand that you're upset, but does everything that happens to you have to be fair? Is it even possible for things to be fair all the time? Are you saying you haven't done *anything* to deserve this treatment? 2. Are you certain you can't stand it? Is it really so awful you'll die? Maybe you're forgetting you're grounded for only a week, not the rest of your life. Does that make a difference?	Still not happy with being grounded, but a bit less angry.

Copping Out

Objective

To recognize avoidance or cop-out behaviors

Materials

Paper and pencils as needed

Procedure

1. Explain that a cop out is when you refuse to take responsibility for yourself and blame others for what happens. Examples might include blaming your coach because you didn't get to start on the team, your parents for grounding you if you got home late, or your friend for ruining your day. Cop outs represent irrational thoughts because you usually want to change the other person rather than take personal responsibility.

2. Avoidance behaviors can involve procrastination, in which you put off doing something because you feel uncomfortable about it or may not want the hassle of doing it. Avoidance may also include behaviors such as ignoring certain people because you don't want to face them, drinking too much to avoid facing a painful or tough situation, overeating or undereating, etc.

3. Invite students to brainstorm personal examples of avoidance or cop-out behaviors.

4. Share examples in small groups (4–5 participants).

Discussion

Content Questions

1. Was it difficult to think of examples of avoidance or cop-out behaviors?
2. Do you think avoidance or cop-out behaviors are healthy or unhealthy?

Personalization Questions

1. How can you recognize cop-out or avoidance behaviors in your own life?
2. What would you like to do about these kinds of behaviors?
3. Do you know others who exercise lots of cop-out or avoidance behaviors? How do you see this affecting their lives? Do you think these behaviors are good?

To the Leader

Help students take personal responsibility for their own behaviors and recognize the unhealthy pattern and effects of avoidance.

Avoidance

Objective

To recognize the beliefs underlying avoidance behavior

Materials

Paper and pencils as needed

Procedure

1. Review the main points from Grades 9–10 Beliefs and Behavior Activity 1 (Copping Out). Emphasize the fact that irrational beliefs underlie avoidance behaviors. Such beliefs might include the following.

   Things should always go my way.

   I shouldn't have to work too hard for things.

   Others should help me take responsibility for my behavior.

   It's easier to avoid responsibilities and problems than to face them.

2. Ask students to pair up and identify five examples of avoidance behaviors and the beliefs they think underlie these behaviors. Encourage them to think of their own behavior, as opposed to that of others.

3. Invite students to share examples.

Discussion

Content Questions

1. Do you see a lot of avoidance behaviors among your peers? What are some of the most common ones?

2. What are the irrational beliefs you think contribute most to avoidance behavior?

Personalization Questions

1. Do you see yourself using avoidance behaviors? How do you feel about this? Share examples.

2. Do you want to keep your avoidance behaviors? If not, what do you plan to do about it?

To the Leader

Encourage students to see the connection between irrational beliefs and avoidance behaviors by pointing out the unrealistic nature of "having to have things be easy."

Why Cop Out?

Objective

To evaluate the advantages and disadvantages of avoidance and cop-out behaviors

Materials

None

Procedure

1. Review the concept of avoidance and cop-out behaviors from Grades 9–10 Beliefs and Behavior Activities 1 and 2 (Copping Out, Avoidance). Emphasize the fact that, even though irrational beliefs underlie these behaviors, people might continue to use them because they see advantages in doing so.

2. Brainstorm with students some advantages of cop-out or avoidance behaviors. For example:

> If you blame your coach for not letting you play first string, you might feel better about your abilities.

> If you break up with someone rather than work through the problems in the relationship, you might avoid having to make changes.

> If you drink to avoid the problems of your parents' divorce, you might postpone having to face painful issues.

> If you eat too much and become overweight, you might not have to worry about competing for dates.

3. Ask students to identify examples of advantages for their own cop-out or avoidance behaviors. Then have them think of the disadvantages: These behaviors can become patterns and you may never learn to face the problems in your life, or you may develop even worse problems by trying to avoid the ones you have.

Discussion

Content Questions

1. Which do you think outweighs the other—advantages or disadvantages of avoidance or cop-out behavior?

Personalization Questions

1. What role have avoidance or cop-out behaviors played in your life or in the life of someone you know?

2. What are some of the advantages or disadvantages of some of your avoidance or cop-out behaviors?

3. What have you learned from this activity, and how can you apply it?

To the Leader

It is very important to help students see that, although there may be short-term advantages to avoidance behavior, in the long run there are only disadvantages.

Tolerating Frustration

Objective

To develop techniques for tolerating frustration

Materials

Paper and pencils as needed

Procedure

1. Ask students to explain the meaning of *frustration* (a sense of dissatisfaction resulting from unresolved problems or unfulfilled needs) and to identify in writing two examples of things that are or have been frustrating to them. Examples might include learning to do something new, trying out but not making a team, struggling with difficult homework assignments, having a conflict of interest with parents or friends, etc. Share examples.

2. Introduce the idea of using *self-talk* to deal with frustration. For example, if you are learning to do something new, you can tell yourself you can't expect to know how to do it the first time and that doing it doesn't have to be easy. In trying out but not making a team, you can tell yourself that not being chosen doesn't mean you are no good, that not everyone makes it, or that maybe it's better to try and not make it than not to try at all.

3. Have students pair up and discuss self-talk they could use to deal more effectively with their own frustrating situations.

4. Share examples in the larger group.

Discussion

Content Questions

1. What is self-talk? How does it apply to frustration?

Personalization Questions

1. Do you ever experience frustration? Under what kinds of circumstances?

2. Have you ever used self-talk in dealing with your own frustrations? If so, how did it work?

3. Does it seem useful to apply self-talk to your frustrating situations? If so, do you anticipate any problems in executing the process? What do you think will be the result?

To the Leader

Self-talk is an essential tool for dealing with frustration. Emphasizing the irrational beliefs that underlie frustrating situations will help students begin to ask the challenging questions needed to cope.

Alternatives to Aggression

Objective

To explore alternatives to aggression

Materials

Newspaper clippings illustrating examples of aggressive behaviors (murder, rape, robbery, spouse or child abuse, etc.)

Procedure

1. Discuss the meaning of *aggression* (a forceful action designed to gain domination).
2. Have students form groups of three. Distribute the newspaper clippings, asking students to identify the examples of aggressive behavior.
3. Next have students discuss what feelings people who behave aggressively might have (anger, defeat, discouragement, revenge, etc). They might talk about what they think motivates people to behave aggressively and what the payoffs for that kind of behavior are.
4. Invite students to brainstorm alternatives to aggression. Instruct them to look at the feelings that precipitate aggressive behavior and to consider alternative ways of dealing with these feelings.
5. Share ideas in the larger group.

Discussion

Content Questions

1. Do you think most people have thought about alternatives to aggressive behavior?
2. Do you think aggressive behavior is good or bad?

Personalization Questions

1. Have you used any alternatives to aggressive behavior? If so, how have they worked for you?
2. Do you have a problem with aggression? If so, what do you think you can do about it?

To the Leader

Students need to recognize that aggressive behavior is a choice they can exercise control over. Putting these suggestions into action is a first step in overcoming a problem with aggression, if one exists.

Be Assertive!

Objective

To learn assertive behavior skills

Materials

Be Assertive Worksheets (Handout 15); pens or pencils as needed

Procedure

1. Discuss the following definitions of *assertion, aggression,* and *nonassertion.*

   Assertion: Standing up for your rights without violating the rights of others. Assertion takes into account the other person's feelings and is not a negative confrontation. Assertion is an appropriate expression of one's feelings, beliefs, and opinions. An assertive person has direct eye contact and a confident manner.

   Aggression: Stating your position in a dominating, humiliating way. Aggression doesn't take into account the other person's feelings or rights. It is an attack on the other person.

   Nonassertion: Being afraid to stand up for your rights or express your opinions. Nonassertive people want to avoid conflict. They keep their feelings bottled up inside but are often very angry because they are allowing themselves to be stepped on by others. Nonassertive people tend to have little eye contact and are shy, unsure of themselves, and indirect.

2. Clarify these definitions and distribute the Be Assertive Worksheets (Handout 15). Students may work individually or with a partner to complete the examples.

3. Share responses.

4. Ask volunteers to role play the situations, having different people assume the assertive, aggressive, and nonassertive roles. Ask one person to act as the recipient of the various messages. Instruct the recipient to respond in a genuine fashion to the different types of messages.

5. Discuss which responses are most effective.

Discussion

Content Questions

1. Was it difficult to distinguish between assertive, aggressive, and nonassertive responses?

2. What do you see as the primary difference between the three types?

Personalization Questions

1. Which do you tend to be in most situations—assertive, aggressive, or nonassertive? Which would you like to be?

2. Which response do you think is most powerful, and why?

3. How can you learn to be more assertive?

To the Leader

You might follow this activity with day-to-day feedback to students on which type of behavior you see them using. Help them see that assertive behavior has the greatest payoffs; aggressive behavior usually results in angry confrontation, and nonassertion typically results in bottled up feelings and negative impact on relationships over time.

HANDOUT 15

Be Assertive Worksheet

Directions: Decide which responses are assertive (AST), aggressive (AGG), or nonassertive (NON). Label them accordingly.

1. Situation: Your parents tell you they don't want you to stay out past 1 a.m. on weekends, and you aren't pleased with the decision.

    _____ Response 1: You say nothing but are really angry and consider staying out later anyway.

    _____ Response 2: You confront your parents, saying that everyone else gets to stay out later and that they are just mean and old fashioned. You say you hate living in their prison and you don't see why they have to make life so miserable for you.

    _____ Response 3: You tell your parents you think that, because you are 16, you should be able to stay out later at least once in a while. You ask them nicely if they will consider letting you do it sometimes.

2. Situation: Your boyfriend or girlfriend stands you up.

    _____ Response 1: You call him/her and say firmly, but not in an angry tone, that you are upset that he/she didn't call and don't like to be treated like that. You tell him/her that, if there is a problem in the relationship, you'd like to discuss it but that you don't want to be treated so disrespectfully.

    _____ Response 2: You call him/her and, in an angry tone of voice, say that he/she is the most inconsiderate person you have ever dated, that you never want to see him/her again, and that you think he/she is a real jerk.

    _____ Response 3: You don't say anything, but you are upset and act very cool and aloof the next time you see him/her. When he/she asks you what the matter is, you say nothing is wrong.

3. Situation: You get a bad grade on a test, and you think that the teacher was unfair in grading it.

    _____ Response 1: You do nothing about it.

    _____ Response 2: You ask the teacher nicely if you could discuss the test. You indicate that you think your answer to the first question is right and request politely that he or she reconsider the response and the grade.

    _____ Response 3: You push your paper in front of the teacher and angrily accuse him or her of being unfair. You tell the teacher that you want your answer looked at again because you know you are right.

PROBLEM SOLVING/
DECISION MAKING

Signs of Stress

Objective

To recognize signs of stress and to consider what these might mean

Materials

Signs of Stress Worksheets (Handout 16); pens or pencils as needed

Procedure

1. Discuss what *stress* is (feeling overwhelmed by circumstances and not knowing how to cope adequately). Indicate that stress is very common and that, when a person is under stress, it is usually more difficult to solve problems and make decisions.

2. Distribute the Signs of Stress Worksheets (Handout 16) and ask students to read and place a checkmark next to those items they have experienced frequently, sometimes, or not at all.

3. Share responses in small groups (4–5 participants).

Discussion

Content Questions

1. Were you aware of these signs of stress?
2. Were you surprised at how you checked the various signs?
3. Are there other signs you have experienced that could be added to the list?

Personalization Questions

1. How do you feel about the number of signs of stress you checked?
2. What does it mean if you do frequently experience a number of these signs?
3. How might this information be useful to you?

To the Leader

It is important for students to realize that the number of signs and the frequency with which they are experienced determine whether or not someone is under stress. In other words, one sign experienced frequently might not be much to worry about; several signs experienced frequently and for quite a while might indicate a problem.

Signs of Stress Worksheet

Directions: Check the appropriate category depending on how often you experience the sign.

1. Inability to get to sleep or restless sleep.

   Frequently _____ Sometimes _____ Not at all _____

2. Irritable, moodier than usual.

   Frequently _____ Sometimes _____ Not at all _____

3. Decrease or increase in eating.

   Frequently _____ Sometimes _____ Not at all _____

4. Increase in drugs or drinking.

   Frequently _____ Sometimes _____ Not at all _____

5. Sudden impulse to cry.

   Frequently _____ Sometimes _____ Not at all _____

6. Worrying about lots of things.

   Frequently _____ Sometimes _____ Not at all _____

7. Lack of control, yelling, lack of patience.

   Frequently _____ Sometimes _____ Not at all _____

8. Confusion, uncertainty.

   Frequently _____ Sometimes _____ Not at all _____

9. Headaches, tension in body.

   Frequently _____ Sometimes _____ Not at all _____

10. Agitated, reckless behavior.

    Frequently _____ Sometimes _____ Not at all _____

11. Decline in achievement.

    Frequently _____ Sometimes _____ Not at all _____

12. Difficulty getting along with others.

    Frequently _____ Sometimes _____ Not at all _____

13. Constant complaining, feeling that things aren't right.

    Frequently _____ Sometimes _____ Not at all _____

14. Listlessness, loss of interest in things.

    Frequently _____ Sometimes _____ Not at all _____

15. Constant demand for perfection in self or others.

    Frequently _____ Sometimes _____ Not at all _____

What Makes It Stressful?

Objective

To identify situations and irrational thoughts that contribute to stress

Materials

Paper and pencils as needed

Procedure

1. Review the material from Grades 9–10 Problem-Solving/Decision-Making Activity 1 (Signs of Stress). Then ask each student to write down a situation he or she would consider to be stressful. Examples could be such things as taking the PSAT exam, parents' fighting, problems with a job, not having enough money, etc. Invite students to share examples.

2. Explain how irrational thinking contributes to stress. Use the example of hating a job: Since someone else could love the same job, what you are telling yourself about the job must contribute to your feeling stressed and angry about it. You might be saying that you shouldn't have to do such hard work, that it is terrible that you have to work on Friday nights, that it is awful to have to get up early on Saturdays, and that you should be able to have money without working so hard. When you think all these thoughts, you are bound to feel negative and become stressed about the situation.

3. Illustrate how changing thoughts can change feelings and result in less stress. Contrast the negative thinking already discussed with the following ideas: I want the money; therefore, maybe I have to put up with the inconvenience of having to work occasionally on Friday nights and early on Saturdays. It would be nice if my parents had enough money so that I didn't have to work, but since they don't I might as well get used to it.

4. Have students write down some irrational thoughts about the stressor they have identified and then try to think of some rational thoughts that would diminish the intensity of the negative feeling and lessen stress.

Discussion

Content Questions

1. Were you able to identify your irrational thoughts about your stressor?
2. What effect, if any, did changing the irrational thoughts to rational ones have on the stressor?
3. What is the connection between stressors and irrational beliefs?

Personalization Questions

1. Have you ever used rational thinking as a means of reducing negative stressors? If so, how did it work?
2. How do you see this strategy as being helpful to you?

To the Leader

Rational thinking can be a good means of reducing the intensity of a stressor and helping put the stressful situation in better perspective. Students may need a good deal of direction in identifying and challenging the irrational thoughts that contribute to stressful situations.

Stress Management

Objective

To learn to distinguish between healthy and unhealthy stress management techniques

Materials

Stress Management Worksheets (Handout 17); pens or pencils as needed

Procedure

1. Discuss the fact that there are healthy and unhealthy ways to deal with stress. Distribute the Stress Management Worksheets (Handout 17) and instruct students to underline the parts of the story they consider to be techniques of handling stress.

2. Have students share the stress management techniques they identified. Write these on the chalkboard. Once they are listed, discuss which ones students think are healthy and which they think are unhealthy. Compile two separate lists.

Discussion

Content Questions

1. How do you distinguish between healthy and unhealthy stress management techniques?

2. Could other stress management techniques be added to either list? Share examples.

3. As a rule, when people are under stress, do you think they use healthy or unhealthy coping techniques?

Personalization Questions

1. Have you ever used any of these techniques to handle stress? Do you tend to use more of the healthy or unhealthy techniques? Share.

2. What have you learned from this lesson that you can use to help you manage stress?

To the Leader

Students need to understand that unhealthy stress management techniques are not in their own best interests because they frequently lead to more stress or stress of a different nature. Using healthy techniques can reduce stress without creating new problems.

HANDOUT 17

Stress Management Worksheet

Directions: Underline each of the stress management techniques as they appear in the following story.

Tim has been experiencing a lot of stress lately because his parents have been fighting. He thinks they might get a divorce. His dad has been drinking a lot and seldom comes home. Tim has been having a hard time getting to sleep, and his grades have been slipping. He has been staying out later with his friends and doing some drinking himself as a way of getting his mind off things. He has been afraid to ask his folks for money, so last week, when he was out of money and his friends wanted to go drinking, he lifted a six-pack from the supermarket. He has lost his temper a lot with his girlfriend, so things aren't so great with her. He got so mad that he almost hit her hard last night. Things just seem to be getting worse instead of better. He finally talked to one of his friends, who suggested that he try jogging, which he intends to do this weekend. He also borrowed a relaxation tape from a friend because he thinks that might help him sleep better. Yesterday he went to the school counselor and talked a little bit about the problems he has been having.

Action or Reaction

Objective

To distinguish between acting and reacting when confronted with problem situations

Materials

Action or Reaction Worksheets (Handout 18); pens or pencils as needed

Procedure

1. Discuss the concept of acting or reacting to problem situations by emphasizing that reacting means you don't anticipate the problem and therefore react to it after it has occurred. Acting, on the other hand, involves anticipating a problem, taking steps to prevent the problem from occurring, or minimizing its effects by taking certain preventative actions.

2. Have students pair up. Distribute an Action or Reaction Worksheet (Handout 18) to each pair, using the first example to illustrate the difference between these two responses. (In the situation as written, Tina is acting; she would be reacting if she didn't think ahead and had to ride with others who have been drinking.) Instruct pairs to complete the remainder of the worksheet on their own.

3. Discuss responses in the larger group.

Discussion

Content Questions

1. Was it difficult to distinguish between acting and reacting? How would you describe the difference between the two?

2. Which do you think people usually do in problem situations—act or react? Which do you think is best?

Personalization Questions

1. Which do you find yourself doing in problem situations—acting or reacting? Which would you rather do?

2. Have you ever acted or reacted in a particular situation? Describe the situation and the results.

To the Leader

If students can see that anticipating problem situations and acting rather than reacting results in a better outcome, they will be more likely to think ahead.

HANDOUT 18

Action or Reaction Worksheet

Directions: Read each of the following situations. Decide if the person was acting (A) or reacting to the situation (R).

_____ 1. Tina has been invited to a party. She knows that a lot of the kids who are going are pretty heavy drinkers. She decides that she will go but will drive her own car so she doesn't have to depend on someone who has been drinking to give her a ride home.

_____ 2. John overheard his parents talking about going out of town for the weekend. He decides not to tell any of his friends because he is afraid they will come over to have a party and trash his house.

_____ 3. You've got a big test in algebra next week. On Wednesday, your friend's parents invite you to go skiing Saturday and Sunday. Even though you could study Wednesday or Thursday, you don't. On Monday, you don't feel prepared to take the test.

_____ 4. Erin hasn't been doing very well in school because her job is taking up a lot of her time. Despite the fact that she has some big projects coming up, she doesn't talk to her boss about cutting back on hours.

_____ 5. Cheerleading tryouts are next week. Susie knows the competition will be pretty stiff, so she is already telling herself that she might not make it and that it won't be so terrible if she doesn't.

_____ 6. A bunch of kids are talking about cruising around in a rough neighborhood to see if they can stir up some excitement. When they ask you to go along, you hop in.

Solutions

Objective

To differentiate between healthy and unhealthy solutions to problems

Materials

Paper and pencils as needed

Procedure

1. Initiate discussion by reading the following situation.

   > Sara has been feeling very rejected by her friends lately. The guy that she had been going with decided not to date her anymore. She has let her schoolwork slide and has pretty much limited her eating to lettuce, rice cakes, and diet pop. She is exercising a lot more and isn't spending much time around anyone.

2. Discuss what Sara is doing and whether or not it is a healthy or unhealthy way to cope with her problems. Then divide students into small groups (3–4 participants) and have them brainstorm some additional unhealthy and healthy ways to solve problems.

3. After 10–12 minutes, have groups share their unhealthy and healthy responses. List responses on the chalkboard.

Discussion

Content Questions

1. Which was easier to think of—healthy or unhealthy responses?
2. Which kind of response do you see kids your age using more often?
3. Do you think it is possible to change from unhealthy to healthy ways of responding to problems?
4. What do you see as the long-term effects of responding to problems in an unhealthy manner?

Personalization Questions

1. Have you generally responded to problems in a healthy or unhealthy way?
2. If you have responded in an unhealthy way, what do you think has prevented you from changing those patterns to healthier ones?

To the Leader

It is important for students to realize that they really do have choices in terms of how they deal with problem situations and that unhealthy responses can frequently lead to more problems.

Ripple Effects

Objective

To recognize the impact decisions made at a single point in time have on subsequent events

Materials

None

Procedure

1. Review the material from Grades 9–10 Problem-Solving/Decision-Making Activity 5 (Solutions) about healthy and unhealthy responses to problems. Emphasize the *ripple effect* of decision making by reading the following.

   > Sara decided that, because she wasn't getting along well with her friends and because her boyfriend had decided not to go out with her anymore, she would limit her eating and not put any more effort into her schoolwork. At first, these decisions didn't have much of an effect—her grades slipped some, as did her weight. But, after about 6 weeks, she was eating much less, her parents were on her about this, and she found that she was obsessed with having to get exercise. Several days in a row she skipped school because she felt she needed to run a lot to work off the pizza she planned on eating at a school party later in the week. However, because she had skipped school, she was suspended from extracurricular activities and couldn't go to the party anyway. Also, because she was so far behind in her schoolwork, she didn't make the honor roll. Her parents told her this would probably have an effect on her getting into college. As time went on, Sara's eating patterns became such a problem that she had to be hospitalized. She was sent away from home to a larger city and couldn't come home until her eating patterns stabilized.

2. Discuss some of the things that happened to Sara because of the way in which she chose to deal with her initial problems. Stress the effect a decision at one point in time has on future consequences.

Discussion

Content Questions

1. What is the ripple effect? Do you see it happening to people you know?
2. What can be done to prevent the ripple effect?
3. Do you think Sara had a choice and could have prevented the ripple effect?

Personalization Questions

1. Have you ever experienced a ripple effect from decisions you made in an attempt to solve a problem? Were the consequences long term? Were there lots of negative implications?
2. What can you do to prevent the ripple effect?

To the Leader

Emphasize the importance of thinking ahead in order to prevent the ripple effect of unhealthy solutions to problems.

INTERPERSONAL
RELATIONSHIPS

Mad at 'Em

Objective

To recognize that negative feelings towards others come from irrational beliefs and that challenging these beliefs can reduce the intensity of these feelings

Materials

Paper and pencils as needed

Procedure

1. Introduce the activity by explaining that feeling angry, upset, and frustrated are common emotions experienced in relation to other people. When we experience these negative feelings, we may fail to recognize where the feelings come from, and as a result may overreact to a situation or stay mad at someone for a long time, thus jeopardizing the relationship.

2. Ask students to write down a situation in which they have felt angry, upset, or frustrated with another person. Illustrate by writing a personal example on the chalkboard, explaining the beliefs about the person or situation that contributed to your negative feelings. For example, if you became angry at your spouse because he forgot to do the grocery shopping, you might have been telling yourself that he never does anything right; that you can't stand the inconvenience; that, if he really cared about you, he would have remembered; and that it's not fair that you have to do all the work all the time.

3. Invite students to discuss their incidents and the beliefs behind their feelings. Point out that, if we didn't have those beliefs, we might not have as many negative feelings. Remind students that it is important to look realistically at the beliefs that contribute to these feelings.

4. Take several of the students' examples and work through the process of challenging beliefs. To illustrate, you could complete the challenges for the example you shared: Instead of telling yourself your spouse doesn't care enough for you to do the shopping, you could consider the fact that maybe he ran out of time, realize that whether or not he does the shopping has nothing to do with his feelings for you, and/or tell yourself it isn't as though he *always* forgets or that you always have to do *all* the work. Stress that replacing irrational with rational beliefs generally results in a less intense negative feeling.

5. Have students pair up and help each other work out challenging questions to help dispel the irrational beliefs behind their negative feelings.

Discussion

Content Questions

1. What was the result of challenging your beliefs? What effect did it have on your anger?

2. How can you distinguish between what is realistic to expect of someone and what is irrational and contributes to negative feelings? (Challenging the belief often makes clear what is unrealistic and what is reasonable.)

Personalization Questions

1. Next time you feel upset, angry, or frustrated towards another person, what is the first thing you need to do? (Identify your beliefs about the person or situation.)

2. What is the next thing you need to do? (Challenge these beliefs to determine what is rational and irrational.)

3. How do you see this procedure affecting your relationships with others?

To the Leader

Understanding the connection between beliefs and negative feelings towards others can help students better control their anger and frustration.

Dependent and Independent Relationships

Objective

To distinguish between dependent and independent behavior in relationships

Materials

Paper and pencils as needed

Procedure

1. Introduce this activity by discussing the difference between dependence and independence. Dependence means that you rely on someone else for support or existence. Independence means that you rely on yourself for support. If you are independent, you are generally more confident of your abilities, more self-reliant, and more in control of yourself.

2. Write the words *dependent* and *independent* on the chalkboard. Engage in a group brainstorming session to identify dependent and independent behaviors in relationships with others. List these under two separate columns on the board. Examples of dependent versus independent behaviors might be sitting at home by the phone waiting for someone to call instead of finding something else to do, or constantly asking for reassurance about whether or not someone likes you as opposed to feeling confident about your self-worth.

3. Discuss whether or not anyone is totally dependent or independent, or whether this depends on the person or the circumstance. Draw a line on the board to illustrate a continuum. Put the word *dependent* on one end and the word *independent* on the other. Have students draw their own continuum on a piece of paper and mark it to identify whether they are more independent or dependent in the following areas: being in dating relationships, going to new places, and meeting new people.

4. Encourage students to generate more areas in which they could express dependence or independence. Have them mark the continuum for each area they suggest.

Discussion

Content Questions

1. How can you distinguish dependent from independent behavior?
2. What did you learn about the different ways dependent behavior is shown?

Personalization Questions

1. In general, do you think you are more dependent or independent in relationships? How do you feel about this?
2. Are there some areas that are more difficult for you than others?
3. Which type of behavior do you think is healthier for you in your relationships with others?

To the Leader

By considering examples of dependent and independent behaviors, students will see that they do have choices in how they respond. It is also important to look at how comfortable students are with the type of behavior they exhibit.

Independent Behavior and Beliefs

Objective

To identify beliefs that interfere with independent behavior in relationships

Materials

Paper and pencils as needed

Procedure

1. Begin by reviewing the definition of independent behavior and the examples generated from Grades 9–10 Interpersonal Relationships Activity 2 (Dependent and Independent Relationships). Contrast these two types of behavior, pointing out that it is possible to vary somewhat in the degree of dependence or independence depending on the circumstance.

2. Read the following situation.

   > Tina and Rob have started seeing each other. Rob says that he will call Tina on Saturday, so instead of going shopping with her friends, she waits around home for him to call. About 5:00 p.m., Gary calls and asks Tina to go to a movie. It is one she would really like to see, but she says no and stays home, getting more miserable by the minute. Rob never calls.

3. Discuss whether or not Tina's behavior is dependent or independent and whether her decision to stay at home and wait was helpful to her in any way. Encourage students to recognize the beliefs that influenced Tina's dependent behavior. Specifically, Tina might feel she had to be approved of by Rob, or that if he called and she weren't there, he might reject her, and that would be awful. She also might believe that her rights don't really count or that others are more important than she is. Point out that behind dependent behavior is usually low self-esteem, lack of assuredness, insecurity, or a need for others to make you feel "whole" or worthwhile.

4. Have students identify a recent situation in which they think they behaved in a dependent fashion. Ask them to identify beliefs they think interfered with their ability to be independent. Share examples.

Discussion

Content Questions

1. What are some examples of beliefs that interfere with independent behavior?
2. If you have these beliefs, is there anything you can do about them?

Personalization Questions

1. How comfortable do you feel with your dependent or independent behavior? What, if anything, would you like to change?
2. If you do want to change, what role do you think your beliefs play?

To the Leader

Independent behavior can be learned. If students are aware of interfering beliefs, there is a greater possibility that they can work on what is blocking them.

Resolving Relationship Issues

Objective

To identify techniques to handle interpersonal relationship difficulties

Materials

Paper and pencils as needed

Procedure

1. Have students pair up and briefly brainstorm examples of relationship problems they have had with others in the past 3 months. These could include problems with peers, parents, teachers, employers, etc.

2. Invite students to share examples of these difficulties. List them on the chalkboard, categorizing them as follows: peer, parent, stepparent, sibling, employer, teacher/principal, police, etc. (Use additional categories as they become apparent.)

3. Next encourage students to brainstorm methods they have used to resolve these difficulties. List alternatives beside the categories to which they correspond so that, ultimately, you can determine which methods work best with which problems.

4. Once all ideas have been generated, go back and discuss pros and cons of the methods suggested, making sure to help students assess the consequences of the various alternatives.

Discussion

Content Questions

1. Which alternatives seem most viable to you?

2. Do certain methods work with one type of problem but not with another? Why do you suppose that is?

3. Do you think there is always a way to resolve differences in relationships?

Personalization Questions

1. Which of the suggested alternatives have worked best for you? Which have not worked?

2. Have you learned some new alternatives that you might try in resolving relationship issues? Share.

To the Leader

Understanding that alternatives for working out conflicts in relationships exist will empower students to deal more effectively with issues as they arise.

Changing Relationships

Objective

To recognize that relationships with others change over time

Materials

Changing Relationships Worksheets (Handout 19); pens or pencils as needed

Procedure

1. After explaining the objective of the activity, distribute the Changing Relationships Worksheets (Handout 19) and go over the directions. Have students complete the worksheets individually.
2. Once the worksheets are completed, divide students into small groups (3–4 participants) to share examples of the ways in which their relationships with others have changed. After 15 minutes, regroup to discuss the Content and Personalization Questions.

Discussion

Content Questions

1. What are some of the ways your relationships have changed?
2. Do these changes depend on the kind of relationship involved (boyfriend/girlfriend, best friend, parent, etc.)? On how long you have been involved with the person?

Personalization Questions

1. How do you feel about some of the ways in which your relationships with others have changed?
2. Do you think it is possible for a relationship to stay the same forever? Have you ever been in a relationship that didn't change?
3. Have you ever tried to resist change in a relationship? How did you do it, and what happened?
4. What are some of the positive outcomes that result from change in relationships?

To the Leader

Change is inevitable, but people at this age may want to resist it and hold onto relationships. Help them to see that change is both negative and positive. Positive aspects of change might be meeting new people, not limiting themselves to a certain group, or gaining independence from parents and others.

HANDOUT 19

Changing Relationships Worksheet

Directions: Think of some people with whom you have had a relationship. Write those people's names in the first column opposite the number of years you have had the relationship. Also indicate how that person is related to you (cousin, friend, parent, etc.). In the second column, indicate one or two ways in which the relationship has changed over the years.

	Name/relationship to you	How relationship has changed
16–17 years		
12–15 years		
8–11 years		
4–7 years		
1–3 years		
Less than 1 year		

I Want, I Demand

Objective

To differentiate between demanding and wishing in relation to others' values, beliefs, and behavior

Materials

Magazine pictures of people engaging in various activities (playing sports, dancing, socializing, smoking, drinking, going to church, etc.); I Want, I Demand Worksheets (Handout 20); paper and pencils as needed

Procedure

1. Divide students into groups of four and distribute a magazine picture to each member. Ask group members to look at each picture and have one person record what the activity is and what they think the belief or value about that behavior is. For example, if the picture is of a sports activity, then the thing valued might be physical exercise, enjoyment of a sport, or love of competition.

2. Upon completion, have several groups share examples of the beliefs or values illustrated by the pictures.

3. Ask each group member to select two pictures, one that represents a value similar to his or her own and one that represents a value different from the student's. For example, a similar value might be enjoying clothing and fashion; a dissimilar value might be drinking alcohol. Ask students to discuss how they respond to other people who have values different from their own.

4. Following this discussion, elicit ideas from the groups as to how they respond to others whose values are different from theirs: Do they ignore them? Not associate with them? Try to change them? Emphasize that differences in values often create dilemmas and that sometimes people might demand that someone change, whereas at other times they might simply wish that the other person shared the same values.

5. Distribute an I Want, I Demand Worksheet (Handout 20) to each student and have small groups discuss the dilemmas.

Discussion

Content Questions

1. Were you able to identify things you do value as well as things you don't?

2. In the dilemmas, what factors seemed to influence what you would do about the differences in values?

3. What seemed to influence the degree to which you wanted to change someone's values?

Personalization Questions

1. What did you learn from this activity about your values?

2. What is your style—do you tend to try to change others, or do you just wish that their values were different? Do you think you can change what someone else values?

To the Leader

Help students see that whether or not they decide to attempt to change someone else's values depends on how strongly they themselves feel about that value. Clarifying what one's own values are and recognizing that others may have different beliefs are essential.

HANDOUT 20

I Want, I Demand Worksheet

Directions: Discuss the following dilemmas.

1. You are a devout churchgoer, and you think that your beliefs have helped you get through some tough experiences. The person you have just begun to date doesn't share these beliefs. What do you do?

2. You are invited to a party with a group of people you don't normally hang around. You know they will be drinking and driving and you have strong beliefs about that not being OK. You do want to go to the party, though. What do you do?

3. The person you have been dating has really been pushing you to spend the night together. It would involve lying to your parents and probably doing some things sexually that you don't feel comfortable about. What do you do?

4. A kid in your class has announced that she has the answers to a history midterm that is rumored to be very difficult. Your best friend gets the answers. You are concerned because you don't believe in cheating, and you are also afraid your friend will get caught. What do you do?

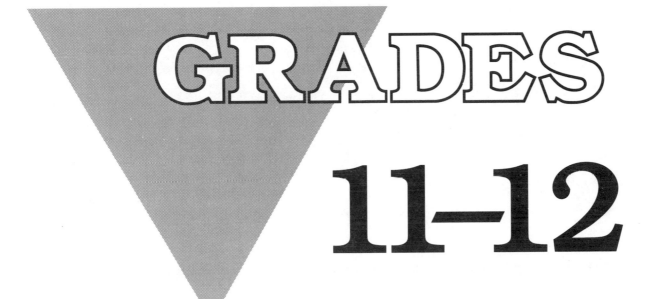

GRADES
11-12

SELF-ACCEPTANCE

Can't Do, Won't Do

Objective

To learn to challenge "I can't" thinking

Materials

Can't Do, Won't Do Lists (Handout 21)

Procedure

1. Write the following sentences on the chalkboard.

   > I can't help it.
   >
   > I can't do it.
   >
   > I can't go.
   >
   > I'd like to, but I can't.
   >
   > I can't help it—that's just the way I feel.

2. Define what the word *can't* means (an inability to do something or a lack of power and control over one's situation) and discuss in what situations students use these sentences or others like them. Does saying you can't mean that you really have no control over a situation or a feeling, or does it mean that you choose not to do something?

3. Invite students to share some examples of "I can't" thinking and to determine whether "I can't" means that something is impossible under any circumstances, someone is preventing them, or they simply don't want to try. Emphasize the relationship between what students tell themselves about the situation or their abilities and the frequency of saying "I can't."

4. Distribute the Can't Do, Won't Do Lists (Handout 21) and ask students to get into groups of three, designating themselves Player A, B, or C. Player A will read the statement, B responds with "I can't," and C responds with "I won't." Have them share reactions to the can't and won't responses.

Discussion

Content Questions

1. In responding to the situations, did you think that you couldn't or that you wouldn't? What is the difference between these two responses?

Personalization Questions

1. When you say "I can't," what does this mean for you? Do you ever say this when you really mean "I won't?"

2. Does "I can't" thinking have any payoffs for you?

3. What relationship do you see between feeling more powerful as a person and an "I can" mentality?

To the Leader

Students need to be able to differentiate between what they really can't do and what they stop themselves from doing because of what they tell themselves about the situation or their abilities. Sometimes saying "I can't" is a way of avoiding risks that could result in failure.

HANDOUT 21

Can't Do, Won't Do List

Directions: Player A reads the statements. Then B says "I can't," and C says "I won't."

1. Let's go to a movie.

2. Why don't you let your feelings show?

3. Go ahead, get mad.

4. Let's get drunk.

5. Let's steal that shirt.

6. Call her and ask her out.

7. Turn the date down if you don't want to go.

8. Just cheat on the test.

9. Just stand him/her up.

10. Share the secret.

Down and Out

Objective

To develop the ability to challenge negative, self-downing thoughts that lead to depression

Materials

None

Procedure

1. Introduce this lesson by explaining some of the characteristics of depression: feeling sad, being discouraged about the future, feeling like a failure, not getting much satisfaction out of things, losing interest in people and events, not being as productive as usual, having difficulty concentrating, crying more than usual, feeling suicidal, etc. Emphasize the difference between experiencing some of these symptoms some of the time and experiencing a lot of them a good deal of the time. (The latter is the time professional help is needed.)

2. Invite students to share their experiences with depression and explain what they have done to cope. Stress the importance of coping with depression in healthy versus unhealthy ways, pointing out that unhealthy ways can lead to more problems.

3. On the chalkboard, write the phrase *taking a test*. Divide the group in half and have half of the students imagine that they are depressed or feeling really down about taking this test. The other half of the group is not depressed. Elicit from the depressed students what their thoughts are. Write these on the board. Do the same for the half who are not depressed.

4. Discuss the thoughts generated by both groups: The depressed thoughts probably have to do with *self-downing* (thinking that you are stupid, that you'll never pass, that everything you do is worthless). You may also disqualify the positive accomplishments you've made prior to the test or assume that what you do is inferior to what others do.

5. Have students break into small groups (4–5 participants) and share examples of situations that have depressed them and some of the negative thoughts behind their feelings. Share these experiences and thoughts in the larger group.

6. Introduce the idea of challenging these self-defeating thoughts by asking yourself questions such as the following.

   > Are you really stupid if you fail this test?

   > If you fail it, does it mean that you have never done anything worthwhile in this class?

   > Even if you do fail it and others pass, does that mean that you are inferior to them?

   Have students practice challenging thinking for the examples they have shared.

Discussion

Content Questions

1. What do you see as the connection between depressed feelings and self-downing talk?
2. What can be done about self-downing thoughts?

Personalization Questions

1. Have you ever put yourself down when you have felt depressed about a situation? How can the concept of challenging self-downing thoughts help you in future situations?

To the Leader

Low self-esteem is an underlying cause of many adolescent problems. Learning to identify and challenge self-downing thoughts will help students deal with difficult situations.

Personal Power

Objective

To learn to exercise personal power to control reactions to life's circumstances

Materials

Paper and pencils as needed

Procedure

1. Write the word *power* on the chalkboard and discuss what it means (possession of control, authority, or influence). Some students may focus on the negative connotations of power, in which it is used to intimidate or oppress. Emphasize that power can also be used productively and positively. When we exercise personal power, we are usually informed, in control of circumstances, and confident and sure of ourselves. In addition, we generally feel better about the decisions we make.

2. Ask students to write down the following ideas: being asked out, participating on a committee, and being a member of a team. Explain that we may look at these situations as ones in which we don't have much power because someone else is making the decisions. Although it is true that we cannot control other people, we can exercise personal power. For example, as concerns being asked out, you have the power to say no if asked, you have the power to ask the other person if you want to, and you have the power to control your thinking so you don't dwell on whether you'll get asked out or assume that it is the end of the world if you don't. Ask students to identify how they could exercise personal power in the remaining two situations.

3. Invite students to identify on paper two situations in which they did not exercise personal power and two in which they did. Ask them to share these with a partner.

Discussion

Content Questions

1. Were you able to think of situations in which you have exercised personal power?
2. How would you define the word *power* in terms of what you can or cannot personally do?

Personalization Questions

1. Do you tend to use your personal power as much as you can?
2. What are some of the things that prevent you from exercising personal power? What can you do to overcome these obstacles?
3. What have you learned from this activity that will help you be a more powerful person?

To the Leader

Many young people see themselves as powerless. It is important to help them see ways in which they can influence events and exert personal control over their own thoughts and actions.

Avoiding Put-Downs

Objective

To learn to avoid self put-downs when faced with negative circumstances

Materials

Paper and pencils as needed

Procedure

1. Ask students to write down the following ideas: getting pregnant (or getting someone pregnant); performing badly in an athletic, music, or speech event; not being accepted by the college of your choice; and getting in trouble with the law. Next ask them to identify a message they may give themselves about each event. Challenge them to think in particular about messages connected with their sense of self-worth. For example, if you get in trouble with the law, do you think you are doomed to failure or are a bad person?

2. Once these negative messages have been identified, invite students to share examples. They may feel more comfortable sharing first in small groups (3–4 participants) and then presenting the examples to the larger group.

3. Help students see that there is no connection between these events and their self-worth. For instance, although not getting accepted to the college of your choice is disappointing, it does not necessarily mean that you are stupid or no good. It may mean that you could have studied harder and gotten better grades, but it does not mean that you are a bad person.

4. Ask students to share with a partner an example of a negative circumstance in which they have put themselves down. Partners should try to help each other see that what they do is not who they are and that it is important to avoid this type of negative self-evaluation.

Discussion

Content Questions

1. Have you put yourself down a lot when faced with negative circumstances?
2. Just because something negative occurs, does that mean you are a worthless person?

Personalization Questions

1. What can you do next time you find yourself being hard on yourself about a situation?
2. How can you apply what you have learned to events in your own or others' lives?

To the Leader

There is a tendency for people with low self-esteem to evaluate themselves in light of events. It is important to help students see the erroneous nature of this assumption.

Self-Worth

Objective

To identify characteristics of low self-worth

Materials

Self-Worth Checklists (Handout 22); pens or pencils as needed

Procedure

1. Introduce the lesson by discussing the meaning of self-worth (the value one attaches to one's personal identity). Stress that self-worth does not come from others' evaluations of us or from the clothes we wear, the cars we drive, or the people with whom we associate. Indicate that, when people feel good about themselves, they behave in ways that reinforce a sense of self-worth.

2. Have students mark the Self-Worth Checklists (Handout 22) for someone they know who they think feels a low sense of self-worth. Which of the characteristics listed fits this person?

3. Next ask students to mark items that pertain to themselves. Stress that this information will not be shared unless they choose to do so.

Discussion

Content Questions

1. What have you learned about low self-worth?

2. Are there some characteristics on the checklist you don't agree with? Are there others you feel should be added?

Personalization Questions

1. Are you personally experiencing any of these characteristics? How do these characteristics affect your life? (Allow students to volunteer this information or not, as they prefer.)

To the Leader

Even though students may not feel comfortable sharing personal characteristics that relate to low self-worth, just being exposed to this information will be helpful to them. (Have students save their checklists for the next activity.)

Self-Worth Checklist

Directions: Place a checkmark beside the characteristics you see in someone you know and an *X* beside those you yourself may exhibit.

_____ 1. Feeling inadequate, as though you don't fit in.

_____ 2. Feeling guilty; thinking you should be doing more or doing things better; feeling as though you are no good because of things you have done.

_____ 3. Feeling ashamed; being haunted by old events; feeling embarrassed because of things you've done in the past.

_____ 4. Grieving; not being able to get over past regrets; feeling as though it's too late to be happy and worthwhile.

_____ 5. Thinking about suicide; believing you're no good, so why stick around?

_____ 6. Having an eating disorder (being overweight, bulimic, or anorexic); believing you're not worthwhile, so why treat your body well?

_____ 7. Smoking, drinking, abusing drugs; feeling you don't matter, so why treat yourself well?

Affirm Yourself

Objective

To learn to use positive affirmations to increase one's sense of self-worth

Materials

Self-Worth Checklists (Handout 22 from Grades 11–12 Self-Acceptance Activity 5); paper and pencils as needed

Procedure

1. Introduce this lesson by reviewing the characteristics of low self-esteem outlined in Grades 11–12 Self-Acceptance Activity 5 (Self-Worth). Note that people can overcome low self-esteem by examining the messages they give themselves. People with low self-esteem frequently tell themselves that they are no good, that they don't matter, that nothing they do is good enough, etc. Ask students to suggest other low self-esteem messages. Record these on the chalkboard.

2. Ask students to select one of the low self-esteem messages discussed and write it down. Then have them think of the opposite of that message and write that down also. For example, if the low self-esteem message were "You never do anything right," its opposite would be "You can do things right." Invite students to share examples, either in small groups (4–5 participants) or as a whole.

3. Discuss the concept of *affirmations* (saying positive things to yourself to validate your worth as a person). Share examples of affirmations, such as the following.

   > You are important.
   >
   > You are a special person.
   >
   > You do have good ideas.
   >
   > You do matter to other people.
   >
   > You are fun to be with.
   >
   > You are capable.

   These affirmations can be taped on a mirror, put on audiotape to listen to, or just remembered each day. Stress the fact that our society oftentimes isn't very reinforcing and that we hear more negative messages than positive ones.

Discussion

Content Questions

1. Did you have any difficulty thinking of positive messages?
2. Do you give yourself more positive or negative messages?

Personalization Questions

1. Have you ever used affirmations? If so, what is your experience with them? Are they a good way for you to look at yourself more positively?

2. If you put yourself down a lot, what purpose does this serve? Do you think using affirmations might be a way to avoid this tendency?

To the Leader

Affirmations are a way of dealing with low self-worth that can give students permission to look at themselves more positively now, as well as in the future.

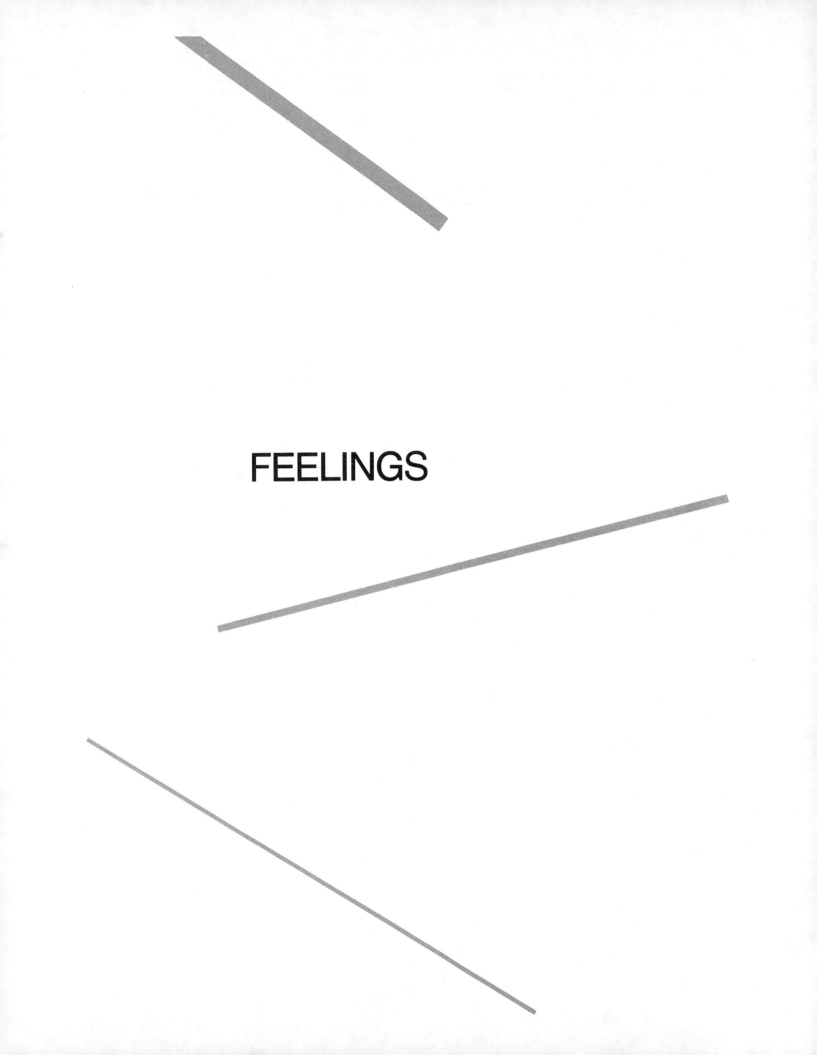

FEELINGS

Defenses

Objective

To learn about how defense mechanisms relate to emotional issues

Materials

Paper and pencils as needed

Procedure

1. Explain that defenses are like walls we put up to keep others out, to make us feel safe, or to help us avoid dealing with feelings or people in a particular situation. Share some examples, such as acting mad when we're scared, drinking too much when we're unhappy, etc.

2. Divide students into small groups (4–5 participants), appoint a recorder per group, and have students brainstorm a list of defense mechanisms that they see themselves, peers, or parents exhibiting. Some of the examples students may generate include acting tough, denying that you're concerned about something, getting angry if someone challenges your beliefs or feelings, etc.

3. Share lists in the larger group.

Discussion

Content Questions

1. Do you think defense mechanisms are used very often? What purpose do they serve?
2. What do you think would happen if we didn't use defense mechanisms?

Personalization Questions

1. Do you find yourself using any defense mechanisms as a way of masking emotions? Share examples.
2. How do you feel about using these defense mechanisms?
3. What's one defense mechanism that you would like to eliminate? How do you think you can do this?

To the Leader

Pointing out how defense mechanisms are used heightens awareness and encourages a more direct approach to problem situations.

Owning Your Emotions

Objective

To recognize who has responsibility for emotions

Materials

Owning Your Emotions Worksheets (Handout 23); pens or pencils as needed

Procedure

1. Introduce this activity by explaining that we often blame others for our feelings or accept responsibility for others' feelings. Although it is important to be sensitive, people must learn how to recognize who "owns" a problem. For instance, if you don't want to go out with someone and that person feels depressed as a result, that person owns the problem, not you. Likewise, if you don't get accepted by the college of your choice, you own the problem of feeling worthless and rejected, not the people who turned you down.
2. Distribute the Owning Your Emotions Worksheets (Handout 23) and give students a few minutes to complete them.
3. Discuss responses, either as a class or in smaller groups of 4–5 students each.

Discussion

Content Questions

1. Who was responsible for most of the emotional problems on the worksheet?
2. Were there any items in particular that you felt were more difficult than others to accept responsibility for?
3. What does it mean to accept ownership of an emotion?

Personalization Questions

1. Have you ever blamed anyone for your emotions or accepted responsibility for another person's feelings?
2. What have you learned about being responsible for emotions?
3. Next time you find yourself shifting responsibility, what can you do about it?

To the Leader

As individuals, we cannot project blame on others for our feelings, nor can we accept undue responsibility for the feelings of others. Learning to own our feelings is one way of encouraging a sense of personal control.

HANDOUT 23

Owning Your Emotions Worksheet

Directions: Decide who owns the problem in the situations described below.

1. You get a bad grade on a paper and blame the teacher because you feel upset about it. Who owns the problem?

2. You turn down a date and later hear that the person went out and got drunk and was really depressed. Who owns the problem?

3. Your parents won't let you stay out until 3:00 a.m. like some of the other kids. You're upset about it. Who owns the problem?

4. Your friend encourages you to take a few drinks, and you do. When you get home, you are grounded. Now you're angry. Who owns the problem?

5. Someone in your class asks if you'll give her the answers for a midterm test. You don't, and the person yells at you. Who owns the problem?

6. You've been dating someone pretty steadily but want to end the relationship. You do. The next day, you hear that the person committed suicide. Who owns the problem?

7. Write your own!

Thoughts and Feelings

Objective

To recognize that emotional problems are caused by thoughts

Materials

Thoughts and Feelings Worksheets (Handout 24); pens or pencils as needed

Procedure

1. After explaining the objective of the activity, distribute the Thoughts and Feelings Worksheets (Handout 24) and have students imagine that the situations listed have occurred. Ask them to identify how they would feel in each case.

2. Share responses to the first situation: Did everyone feel the same way about this event? Explain that feelings don't occur just because something has happened. Rather, we have a particular feeling because of what we think about the situation.

3. Help students identify what they might have been thinking about the first situation. For example, if they were upset and angry, they might have been thinking that the principal is a louse and has no right to do this, that the situation is terrible, and that their lives are ruined because they can't have prom. On the other hand, if they weren't upset, they might be thinking that it doesn't really matter, that proms cost a lot of money and aren't that much fun anyway, or that now no one has to worry about whom to ask. Point out that it is the belief about the event that results in the feeling.

4. Share responses (both feelings and beliefs) to the other situations. Then have students identify and discuss some personal situations of their own.

Discussion

Content Questions

1. If you change your thoughts, what happens to your feelings?
2. Do you think it is possible to change your thoughts about every situation?

Personalization Questions

1. Have you ever changed your feelings about a situation by changing your thoughts? How effective has this been for you?
2. How can you apply the information from this lesson in your daily life?

To the Leader

If students understand the relationship between thoughts and feelings, they will be able to exercise more emotional control over events.

HANDOUT 24

Thoughts and Feelings Worksheet

Directions: Read each of the situations and identify your feelings and thoughts about each.

1. The principal announces that there will be no junior-senior prom.

   Feelings:

   Thoughts:

2. Your parents won't let you apply to the college of your choice.

   Feelings:

   Thoughts:

3. You want to stay in your hometown after graduation so you can be near your friends. Your parents say you can't.

   Feelings:

   Thoughts:

4. The person you've been dating starts seeing someone else.

   Feelings:

   Thoughts:

5. Write your own!

   Feelings:

   Thoughts:

Coping with Painful Feelings

Objective

To identify options for coping with emotional pain

Materials

Various newspaper clippings suggesting ways people deal with painful feelings (advice columns, announcements for self-help or personal growth groups, articles about how terminally ill people cope, news accounts of suicides, etc.)

Procedure

1. Divide students into small groups (3–4 participants) and distribute a couple of articles per group. Ask them to discuss the painful emotions involved and how the individuals involved coped with the pain.
2. Have all groups share the methods of coping and invite them to add their own solutions.

Discussion

Content Questions

1. Do you think some methods of coping are better than others? Why?
2. Do you think most people use a variety of methods or stick to just a few? Which do you think is better?

Personalization Questions

1. Which methods have worked best for you?
2. Have you used any methods that weren't very beneficial? Share.
3. Have you learned about any additional ones that you would like to try?

To the Leader

There are many methods of dealing with emotional issues. It is important to help students evaluate them and recognize that some are more appropriate than others for dealing with the feelings involved in different situations.

Dealing with Depression

Objective

To learn about depression and ways to deal with it

Materials

Dealing with Depression Quizzes (Handout 25)

Procedure

1. Write a definition of the word *depression* on the chalkboard (feeling gloomy, saddened, low-spirited).
2. Distribute the Dealing with Depression Quizzes (Handout 25) and give students time to respond.
3. Discuss responses in small groups (3–4 participants). (All items on the quiz are true.)

Discussion

Content Questions

1. Was it difficult for you to identify the signs and symptoms of depression? Are there any characteristics you would add to the list?
2. What are some of the problems teens have today that contribute to depression?
3. How do you think you can deal with depression?

Personalization Questions

1. Have you ever felt depressed? Are you able to identify signs and symptoms for yourself?
2. If you do get depressed, what do you think you will do to try to deal with your feelings?

To the Leader

Teenage depression is very common, and it is important that students recognize and learn healthy ways to deal with it.

HANDOUT 25

Dealing with Depression Quiz

Directions: Answer the following questions true (T) or false (F).

_____ 1. Changes in eating and sleeping can be a sign of depression.

_____ 2. If you are bored, you could be depressed.

_____ 3. When depressed, you generally feel hopeless.

_____ 4. When depressed, you tend to withdraw from friends.

_____ 5. A sudden change in grades may signal depression.

_____ 6. Being overly self-critical is a symptom of depression.

_____ 7. Kids who act out are sometimes depressed. (Acting out may mean being aggressive, being sexually active, stealing, shoplifting, doing drugs, etc.)

_____ 8. Constant TV watching or being very lazy and lethargic may signal depression.

_____ 9. Driving too fast or participating in risky or dangerous activities may mean a person is depressed.

_____ 10. Talking about suicide usually indicates depression.

In Our Own Best Interests

Objective

To recognize the relationship between feelings and acting in one's own best interests

Materials

Several newspaper clippings or articles about suicide, alcoholism, drug dependency, delinquency, eating disorders, etc.; paper and pencils as needed

Procedure

1. Divide students into groups of four and distribute one article to each group. Indicate that these articles describe ways in which people have attempted to deal with problems in their lives. Ask each group to appoint a recorder, then discuss the following questions.

    What do you think this person's problem is?

    Why do you suppose the person handled the problem in this way?

    What feeling do you think the person with this problem is trying to deal with?

    Do you think the way in which the person is dealing with the problem is positive? Why or why not?

2. Discuss each group's responses to the questions.

Discussion

Content Questions

1. Do you think the methods shown for dealing with these problems are healthy or unhealthy? Identify the healthy ones and the unhealthy ones.
2. Which of these solutions will help a person act in his or her own best interests?

Personalization Questions

1. Have your feelings ever been so overwhelming that you have tried (or contemplated) any of the unhealthy methods?
2. If so, how do you think doing so helped deal with the problem? Did it create any new problems?
3. If you ever feel overwhelmed by feelings again, what are some positive coping strategies you could try?

To the Leader

Students need to recognize that they don't have to be so overwhelmed by feelings that they see only drastic measures as the solution. Helping them look at what is in their own best interests and recognize alternatives is critical.

BELIEFS AND BEHAVIOR

Argue with Yourself

Objective

To develop more flexible behavior by learning to challenge irrational beliefs

Materials

Argue with Yourself Worksheets (Handout 26); pens or pencils as needed

Procedure

1. Distribute one Argue with Yourself Worksheet (Handout 26) per student and discuss an example of a situation that illustrates the first irrational belief. For example, "It's awful if everything doesn't go my way" might be a belief held by a basketball player who was cut from the squad.
2. Divide students into small groups (3–4 participants) and have them write down example situations for the rest of the irrational beliefs. Situations should be based on experiences they or their peers have had.
3. Invite students to share examples.
4. Introduce the concept of challenging beliefs to develop a more rational pattern of thinking and more positive feelings. Challenging involves asking yourself questions that help you look at the situation in a different way. For example, if your parents won't let you go out with a particular person, is it really the end of the world? Is it possible that they do have a good reason for denying the request? Does it mean that they don't care about you if they won't let you go?
5. Practice challenging some of the irrational beliefs listed on the worksheet. Have students write down examples of the challenging questions they can use.

Discussion

Content Questions

1. How can you challenge beliefs? Do you think challenging can do any good?

Personalization Questions

1. Was it difficult to think of situations in which you or someone else had these irrational beliefs, or do you see these happening quite regularly?
2. What has your experience been in challenging irrational beliefs?
3. If you haven't used the challenging technique before, can you see yourself using it?

To the Leader

Depending on what activities students have already experienced, they may be more or less familiar with the challenging technique. If the concept is new to them, model the process several times. (Have students save the worksheet from this lesson for the next activity.)

Argue with Yourself Worksheet

Directions: Write down a situation in which you or someone else may have had the following irrational beliefs. Then write down some challenges for each one.

1. It's awful if everything doesn't go my way.

   Situation:

   Challenges:

2. I shouldn't have to work too hard at anything.

   Situation:

   Challenges:

3. People shouldn't make mistakes.

   Situation:

   Challenges:

4. I should do everything perfectly.

   Situation:

   Challenges:

5. People should be treated fairly.

   Situation:

   Challenges:

6. If others reject me, I must not be any good.

   Situation:

   Challenges:

7. I can't stand being criticized.

   Situation:

   Challenges:

8. If I'm unhappy, it isn't my fault and I can't change it.

   Situation:

   Challenges:

Control Your Impulses

Objective

To develop strategies for controlling impulsive behavior

Materials

Argue with Yourself Worksheet (Handout 26 from Grades 11–12 Activity 1)

Procedure

1. Discuss the definition of *impulsive behavior* (acting suddenly, without thinking through the consequences of the behavior). Brainstorm some examples of impulsive behavior, such as punching someone when angry, hurting yourself, stealing something without thinking about what will happen later, spending large sums of money, etc.

2. Discuss why students think people do things on impulse and what some of the consequences of impulsive behavior are.

3. Introduce the idea that irrational beliefs underlie impulsive behaviors. Such beliefs might include the following.

   > I can't stand it.

   > It's not fair and shouldn't happen to me.

   > I'll get even.

   > Things are rotten anyway, so why try?

   Generate additional possibilities.

4. Review the concept of challenging beliefs as described in Grades 11–12 Beliefs and Behavior Activity 1 (Argue with Yourself). Suggest challenging as a means of dealing with impulsive behavior and use the example situations detailed in Handout 26 to discuss the types of questions one can ask oneself to curb impulsive behavior.

Discussion

Content Questions

1. Do you think impulsive behavior is very common?
2. Are there any payoffs that come from impulsive behavior?
3. What can be done about impulsive behavior?

Personalization Questions

1. Have you had any experience with impulsive behavior? If you do act impulsively, how do you feel about it?
2. Have you ever tried to change your impulsive behavior? If so, what did you try and how did it work?
3. Do you know anyone who is impulsive? What is having a relationship with that person like?

To the Leader

It is critical that students learn to control impulsive behavior so they don't overreact to events and end up making decisions that could have long-term negative consequences.

SDB's

Objective

To define and identify self-defeating behaviors (SDB's)

Materials

Paper and pencils as needed

Procedure

1. Define what is meant by *self-defeating behavior* (behaving in a way that works against oneself or doing things that are not in one's best interests). SDB's might include not eating properly, drinking too much, or blaming yourself for everything.
2. Ask each person to make a list of SDB's for themself or someone they know.
3. In groups of three, have students share their lists, identifying a person to record all ideas on a combined list. From this combined list, they are to select three SDB's they are willing to share with the total group.
4. As behaviors are shared by each small group, have each student compile a list of all the SDB's shared. Students are then to rate each item as it applies to them. The following codes can be written on the chalkboard: N (don't do this at all), S (do this sometimes), and L (do this a lot).

Discussion

Content Questions

1. What did you learn about SDB's?
2. Do you think many people practice these kinds of behaviors?
3. Are SDB's healthy?

Personalization Questions

1. How do you feel about the SDB's you practice (if any)?
2. What would you like to do about the SDB's you have? Have you ever eliminated any? If so, how? What was the result?

To the Leader

Students need to learn that they can act in their own best interests. Identifying SDB's in self or others is a good way to begin understanding sensible behavior.

Believing and Behaving

Objective

To identify irrational beliefs that contribute to self-defeating behaviors (SDB's)

Materials

Paper and pencils as needed

Procedure

1. Ask students to write the following words down the left side of their paper: *who, what, where,* and *why*. Then ask them to write down beside *who* their own name or the name of someone they know who practices some form of SDB. Next have them determine what the SDB is and write that beside *what*. Beside *where,* they are to identify the typical location where the SDB occurs. (For example, if the behavior is overeating, the *where* might be either in restaurants or at home.) The last category is *why*. Students are to write down reasons the identified person engages in the SDB. (For instance, maybe the person eats when upset or to avoid socializing with others.)

2. Without identifying the *who, what,* or *where,* make a composite list of the *why's* by writing responses on the chalkboard. Once the composite list is compiled, examine the reasons and try to determine underlying irrational beliefs. These might include ideas such as the following.

   I can't stand it.

   Poor me.

   Life's too hard.

   Everything should go my way.

   I can't control my feelings or my behavior.

   Other people shouldn't upset me.

3. Discuss the role of self-talk in challenging these beliefs. For example, if a person generally overeats when upset with someone or something, that person may be saying that everything should go the way he or she wants it to and that overeating can't be controlled. Challenging self-talk would help this person realize he or she doesn't have to be upset with what others do and that choices do exist.

Discussion

Content Questions

1. How do you think SDB's "help" a person solve a problem? Is the problem really solved?
2. What is the relationship between SDB's and irrational beliefs?

Personalization Questions

1. If you have any SDB's, which irrational beliefs do you think underlie them?
2. What happens if you substitute healthier (or more rational) beliefs for SDB's?

To the Leader

It is important that students recognize the connection between SDB's and irrational beliefs and understand that challenging beliefs is a good way of eliminating these behaviors.

Defeat the SDB's

Objective

To recognize alternatives to SDB's

Materials

Defeat the SDB's Worksheets (Handout 27); pens or pencils as needed

Procedure

1. Distribute the Defeat the SDB's Worksheets (Handout 27) and ask students to pair up and identify one reason someone might exercise each behavior and one reason that person might not. For example, a person might drink too much because he or she wants to join in but might not in order to avoid the possibility of getting in an accident while drunk.

2. Discuss responses, challenging how sensible the reasons for practicing the various SDB's are.

3. As a group, brainstorm alternatives students can try when they think they might not be acting in their own best interests. Examples include asking for help; talking to a friend, parent, teacher, or counselor; going to self-help groups; using relaxation techniques; reading about the problem; practicing self-talk, etc.

Discussion

Content Questions

1. What did you learn as you identified reasons for and against the practice of SDB's?
2. How do you think SDB's can become a problem?

Personalization Questions

1. Next time you feel like doing something self-defeating, what alternatives do you have?

To the Leader

Students need to see that, although SDB's may seem like a good way to deal with troublesome situations, in reality they may create even worse problems.

Defeat the SDB's Worksheet

Directions: Identify a reason why a person might want to use each of the SDB's listed. Then identify a reason why not.

	Why	**Why Not**
Suicide		
Overeating		
Drug abuse		
Drinking		
Anorexia		
Bulimia		
Driving too fast		
Violence		
Being too dependent in a relationship		
Going along with things you don't really feel comfortable with		

What's Influential?

Objective

To identify positive and negative ways of influencing others' behavior

Materials

What's Influential Worksheets (Handout 28); pens or pencils as needed

Procedure

1. Distribute the What's Influential Worksheets (Handout 28) and have students fill them out.
2. In small groups (3–4 participants), have students discuss the items they agreed with, disagreed with, or were uncertain about.
3. In a total group, determine which items they see as being the most positive methods of influencing someone else.

Discussion

Content Questions

1. How much control do you think you really have over someone else's behavior?
2. What positive means of influencing others exist?

Personalization Questions

1. What is your style of influencing others?
2. If you are trying to influence someone, do you find you are more successful if you use positive or negative methods?
3. What has been your experience in trying to control someone else's behavior? Has doing so worked for you? Were there any payoffs?

To the Leader

Help students see that they do have a choice as to how they attempt to influence someone else. Although there is no guarantee that you can change someone's behavior, the chances of doing so are better if you use a positive method.

What's Influential Worksheet

Directions: Read and mark each item according to whether you agree (A), disagree (D), or are uncertain (U).

_____ 1. It is possible to control someone else's behavior.

_____ 2. Being indirect and hinting about something that is bothering you is better than communicating directly about it.

_____ 3. If you don't like someone else's behavior, you should always let them know.

_____ 4. In order to control someone else's behavior, you must be manipulative and play games like "hard to get," "you're not important to me," and "I'll show you."

_____ 5. Honestly communicating one's feelings may or may not influence others.

_____ 6. It is not possible for everyone to behave as we want them to all of the time.

_____ 7. Threatening or being violent is not a good way to influence others.

_____ 8. Demonstrating positive behavior yourself may be a way of influencing someone else.

_____ 9. If someone is doing something you think is wrong, you have no right to tell them what you think about it. You shouldn't try to influence them.

_____ 10. If you are trying to influence your parents to make a decision about something you want to do, lying a bit doesn't hurt and may be a way to get them to say yes.

PROBLEM SOLVING/
DECISION MAKING

Ideal Solutions

Objective

To recognize that solutions to problems aren't always ideal

Materials

Index cards; pens or pencils as needed

Procedure

1. Discuss the nature of solutions to problems, explaining that sometimes a solution may be one that really works out well and satisfies everyone involved in the problem. At other times, someone has to compromise in order for a solution to be reached. In some cases, a solution is decided upon by someone else (parents or teachers, for example) and may or may not be satisfactory.

2. Distribute one index card per student. Ask students to write down a brief description of a problem they or someone in their family has had and the solution that was reached. Ask them to write *ideal* beside the solution if it was ideal for everyone involved. Students should not put their names on the cards.

3. Collect the index cards and redistribute them at random. Invite some of the students to read aloud the solutions and to indicate whether or not the solution was thought to be ideal.

Discussion

Content Questions

1. Were there lots of ideal solutions?
2. How realistic is it for everyone to be pleased about the solution to a problem?
3. Were some of the identified solutions ones you had not thought of? Are any of them options you could use to help solve some of your problems?

Personalization Questions

1. In your own experience, have more solutions to problems been ideal or not ideal?
2. Do you find yourself using the same solutions over and over, or do you try to be creative and come up with more satisfactory solutions?
3. What is one idea from today's lesson that you can apply to future problem-solving situations?

To the Leader

Realizing that there generally is no ideal solution to a problem may help students understand that some give and take is necessary in order for any solution to occur. They can also benefit from knowing that multiple solutions are possible if they think creatively.

Not a Problem, an Opportunity

Objective

To recognize that problem situations can be turned into opportunities for growth

Materials

Photocopies of newspaper articles about people with problems (athletes who have had drug problems but are now in rehabilitation, teens who have committed crimes, people who have made unsuccessful suicide attempts, etc.)

Procedure

1. Introduce the activity by asking students to think about a time when they or someone they know had a problem but later grew personally from having had it. An example might be a divorce situation, in which ultimately the husband or wife ended up much happier and more self-sufficient. Invite students to share examples.

2. Divide students into groups of four and distribute a photocopy of the same newspaper article to each group member. Students are to read the article and then discuss what the problem was, how the person might have grown from having the problem, and what pain and struggle was involved in the process.

3. Share responses from each small group.

Discussion

Content Questions

1. How realistic do you think it is for growth opportunities to result from a problem situation?

2. How many people do you think take advantage of these growth opportunities and use problems situations to turn their lives around? What obstacles do you think there are in doing this?

Personalization Questions

1. Have you ever experienced a situation in which you have turned a problem into an opportunity? Share.

2. What do you think you can do to encourage people to turn problem situations into opportunities for growth?

To the Leader

It is important for teens to realize that they don't have to ruin the rest of their lives because of a problem at a given point in time. Recognizing the courage it takes to overcome problems is a step in the right direction. Students also need to realize that they can support and encourage their peers to turn problems into opportunities.

Put It in Perspective

Objective

To develop the ability to put problems in perspective

Materials

Paper and pencils as needed

Procedure

1. Discuss the idea of problems sometimes seeming worse than they are at the time they are happening. Point out that it is important to be able to put problems in some sort of perspective to avoid overreacting to a situation that later won't seem so important.

2. List the following ideas on the chalkboard.

   Earthquake

   Friend not phoning you

   Being in an accident

   Not getting asked to a dance

   Taking college entrance tests

   Having someone say an unkind thing about you

   Having someone in your family develop a serious illness

3. Ask students to copy these ideas down and rank order them from most to least important. Invite volunteers to share their highest and lowest ranked items. Discuss similarities and differences.

4. Next ask students to think of some problems they have experienced within the past year. These could be any situations that have affected them, such as a problem with illness in the family, something that happened to a best friend, etc. (Stress that these problems will be kept confidential.)

5. After students have identified several problems, have them assign them the following codes.

   ST: Short-term problem that was resolved fairly easily

   LT: Long-term problem that wasn't readily resolved

   MIN: Minor in comparison to other problems

   MAJ: Major in comparison to other problems

   SW: Seemed worse at the time than it did later

Discussion

Content Questions

1. How many of your problems were short-term as opposed to long-term?

2. How many of your problems were minor as opposed to major in comparison to other problems?

3. How many of your problems seemed worse at the time than they did later?

4. What did you learn from coding your problems?

Personalization Questions

1. Have you ever overreacted to a problem that now seems minor in comparison to others? What do you think you could have done at the time in order to help you put the problem in better perspective?

2. Next time you are faced with a series of seemingly overwhelming problems, what can you do to get a more realistic grasp of the situation?

To the Leader

Putting problems in perspective is an important task for teenagers because they frequently tend to overreact or act impulsively. The consequences of these impulsive decisions can be very detrimental.

Rational or Emotional?

Objective

To differentiate between emotional and rational problem-solving approaches

Materials

Popular songs implying powerlessness and impulsive reactions, as well as more rational reactions (lyrics or audiorecordings); paper and pencils as needed

Procedure

1. Indicate that the objective of the activity is to differentiate between solving problems in a rational manner (in which the situation is thought through) and allowing one's emotions to rule. Distribute the lyrics or play the songs selected. Invite students to write down examples of each type of reaction.

2. Discuss some examples of the two approaches to problem solving noted in the songs. For example, a statement like "I can't live if you don't love me" reflects an emotional approach, whereas a statement like "We can work it out" might be more rational, implying that efforts need to be taken and that one doesn't have to give up. A song espousing drug use as a way to deal with life could be classified as emotional, whereas a song implying that feelings need to be expressed could be classified as rational.

3. After several examples of rational and emotional problem solving have been given, ask students to pair up and brainstorm examples of both approaches from their own or others' experience. Share examples in the total group.

Discussion

Content Questions

1. Which do you think is more common—rational or emotional approaches to problem solving?

2. Which do you think is more effective—rational or emotional approaches to problem solving?

3. What do you think is most difficult about solving problems in rational ways? Do you think if you respond in an emotional manner that you've really solved the problem?

Personalization Questions

1. Do you tend to solve problems emotionally or rationally? Which method has the biggest payoffs for you?

2. If you tend to be more emotional in your problem-solving approach, how do you think you might be able to change? What are the benefits of responding more rationally?

To the Leader

Music is an influential medium for teenagers. Teaching them about the messages conveyed in song lyrics can help them differentiate between rational and emotional approaches and recognize the powerlessness that is often conveyed in popular songs. (To identify songs, listen to a Top 40 radio station or ask a couple of students in advance to help you with this task.)

Goals

Objective

To distinguish realistic from unrealistic goals

Materials

Goals Worksheets (Handout 29)

Procedure

1. Discuss the definition of the word *goal* (the end toward which efforts are directed). Ask students to share examples of goals they have.

2. Explain that the purpose of this activity is to distinguish between realistic, attainable goals and goals that are so broad or unrealistic that they are probably not attainable. A realistic goal would be to complete high school if you have been taking the right number of credits all along. An unrealistic goal would be to expect to graduate with your class if you would have to take eight classes in one term in order to have the right number of credits.

3. Distribute the Goals Worksheets (Handout 29) and have students decide which situations are realistic and which are not.

4. Share responses.

Discussion

Content Questions

1. Was it difficult to distinguish between realistic and unrealistic goals? What is the difference between these two types?

2. Do you think it is possible for a goal that is unrealistic at one point in time to become realistic at another?

Personalization Questions

1. Do your goals seem realistic or unrealistic? If they are unrealistic, what do you think you can do to make them more realistic?

2. Do you see any advantages to having unrealistic goals?

To the Leader

Although dreaming a bit may help people consider all possible future possibilities, realistic, attainable goals are more helpful in the long run because they help students focus their lives, both for the present and the future.

HANDOUT 29

Goals Worksheet

Directions: Read each of the following situations and decide if the person's goals are realistic (R) or unrealistic (U).

_____ 1. Rae wants to go to college. She is in her senior year and has taken 2 years of algebra, no advanced science, and only one advanced English course.

_____ 2. Barbara has acted in several productions in a large high school. She has acted in the community theatre and has taken acting lessons for several years. She is going to New York after graduation to try to get into the theatre.

_____ 3. Linda has a low-paying job in a bank. She and her husband were married right out of high school. He currently works as a mechanic but has changed jobs several times in the past few years. He tells Linda that he has found his calling and that she can plan on his being the head of all the mechanics in the shop within 3 months.

_____ 4. Steve has never worked too hard in school. His grades have been mostly *B*'s and some *C*'s. His dad has always given him plenty of money, so, although he has had a couple of jobs, he has quit after a few weeks because he didn't like the hours or having to give up a good time. Now he is going to college at a Big Ten school. He says he's pretty sure he'll get all A's and can still have a good time.

_____ 5. Tanya has been far behind in all of her work all semester. Now, with a week to go, she says she can not only get all of her work handed in but can get *A*'s on the final exams too. Prior to this semester, her grade point average was a 3.0 on a 4.0 scale.

_____ 6. Eric has always wanted to be a scientist. When he was young, he spent hours with his microscope and chemistry set. In school, he has taken every available science course and has done very well. He is now applying for some science scholarships and thinks he has a good chance of getting one.

How to Decide

Objective

To learn to make decisions that are in one's own best interests

Materials

Paper and pencils as needed

Procedure

1. List the following decisions on the chalkboard.

> Decides to enlist in the army because he can't think of anything else to do.
>
> Decides to go to cosmetology school because all her friends are doing it.
>
> Tries smoking dope because she's afraid kids will make fun of her if she doesn't.
>
> Doesn't stay overnight in a motel with his girlfriend and some other kids because he doesn't feel comfortable doing it.
>
> Has a chance to cheat on a major exam but doesn't because he figures he'll need to know the material later on anyway.

2. After students have read these decisions, discuss which ones illustrate that the person involved was thinking ahead and acting in his or her own best interests. Identify the factors involved in acting in your own best interests: anticipating consequences; doing what feels right for you, even though it may be different from what your peers want you to do; and looking at how you can be in charge of your life as an actor, not a reactor.

Discussion

Content Questions

1. Do you think kids your age usually make decisions that are in their own best interests?
2. If they don't, what do you think prevents them from doing so?
3. What do you see as the payoffs for acting in one's own best interests?

Personalization Questions

1. Is acting in your own best interests a problem for you? If so, what gets in your way, and what can you do about it?
2. How can you apply what you have learned in this lesson to your own life?

To the Leader

Because of the many choices open to youth, it is important that they recognize how to make decisions that are in their own best interests. Doing so may be difficult, but if students realize that they have choices, they may begin to consider the alternatives more carefully.

INTERPERSONAL
RELATIONSHIPS

Change Them?

Objective

To learn that you can't change other people, only your reaction to them

Materials

Change Them Situations Lists (Handout 30); pens or pencils as needed

Procedure

1. Introduce the activity by asking students if they have ever been upset over anything the President of the United States has done. Ask how many of them have been successful in changing the President's beliefs or behaviors. Indicate that the purpose of this activity will be to determine the extent to which we have the power to change other people.

2. Distribute the Change Them Situations Lists (Handout 30). Divide students into groups of three and have them discuss what they would do in each situation.

3. Share responses in the larger group.

Discussion

Content Questions

1. What did you decide to do in each of these situations?

2. Do you think it is really possible to change another person?

Personalization Questions

1. Have you ever tried to change another person? What was your experience?

2. Have you ever tried to change your reaction to another person? How did you go about doing that?

To the Leader

Students at this age often believe they can always have things go the way they wish. It is very important to acknowledge their desire to change other people at the same time helping them assess how realistic this belief is. Assertive communication techniques can help students express their feelings and recognize the limits of their control.

HANDOUT 30

Change Them Situations List

Directions: Decide what you would do if you were in the following situations.

1. Your grandparents have what you consider to be old-fashioned ideas about dating. For example, they think it is inappropriate for girls to call boys, for girls to pay for dates, or for boys and girls to be at someone's house when the parents are not home. If your grandparents had these opinions, what would you do? Would you try to change their opinions? Or would you change the way you react to their ideas?

2. Your best friend was in Europe over the summer and came back with some very strong religious ideas that she had gotten from some fellow travelers. She has shared some information with you and has invited you to go to church with her. You really think she is getting carried away with her ideas. What do you do? Try to change her? Go along with her? Try to change the way you react to her?

3. A friend of yours is pregnant and is getting an abortion. You don't believe in abortion, and the situation is really upsetting to you. You have tried talking to your friend, but she won't change her mind. What do you do? Would you keep talking? Stop being her friend because of your differences in values? Realize that you have differences but that you can't change her?

4. You used to run around with a group of kids who drank beer and smoked cigarettes. You did these things, too, but made the decision that you didn't want to continue. Now you are really upset that the others in the group don't feel the same way you do. Can you try to convince them to stop? Should you stop being friends with them? Should you change your behavior and start drinking and smoking cigarettes again?

5. One of your friends is going out with a person you think is a really bad influence. You try to talk to your friend, but he won't listen—he swears he can change this girl and that he knows what he is doing. Do you try to convince him that he will get hurt and that he shouldn't see her? Do you let him do what he wants to do about the relationship? Do you stop being his friend because he won't see what he is doing to himself?

Negative Feelings towards Others

Objective

To recognize the connection between negative feelings towards others and irrational beliefs about them

Materials

Paper and pencils as needed

Procedure

1. Ask students to think of a time when they have had negative feelings about someone with whom they have had a relationship. Then ask them to identify what was negative about the relationship and how they felt (for example, feeling angry because a boyfriend or girlfriend wasn't home when expected).

2. Next review the concept of irrational beliefs, pointing out that such beliefs are characterized by *shoulds* about how another person must act, awfulizing, overgeneralizing, or putting oneself down unncessarily. Discuss the connection between negative feelings in relationships and irrational beliefs. For example, finding out a boyfriend or girlfriend isn't home when expected might not be upsetting to everyone. But it might be upsetting if you overgeneralized and assumed the situation meant the person was with someone else, that you didn't matter, or that the person had lied to you. When you think irrationally, you don't stop to consider that maybe something unforeseen prevented the person from being home and that the event in itself really isn't anything to get upset about.

3. Have students discuss, in pairs, how negative feelings in relationships may relate to irrational beliefs.

Discussion

Content Questions

1. How can irrational beliefs influence feelings about relationships?

Personalization Questions

1. What connections do you see between your own negative feelings in relationships and irrational beliefs? Share examples.
2. How do you think your relationships might change if your beliefs about the relationship changed?
3. What can you apply from this activity to your present relationships?

To the Leader

Stressing the connection between beliefs and feelings in relationship situations is a means of helping students see that they don't have to be controlled by negative feelings. Understanding this idea will help them deal with peers as well as adults.

Self-Talk

Objective

To learn to utilize self-talk to reduce negative emotionality in relationships

Materials

Paper and pencils as needed

Procedure

1. Review the material from Grades 11–12 Interpersonal Relationships Activity 2 (Negative Feelings towards Others) on the connection between irrational beliefs and negative feelings in relationships. Ask students to write down one negative relationship experience and to identify the feeling and the associated irrational beliefs. For example, suppose your parents won't let you use the car because the last time you used it you didn't go to the library, where you said you were going, but rode around town instead. Now you feel angry and are telling yourself that they should let you take the car, they never trust you, they always deny you, it will ruin your weekend if you can't have the car, and that the situation is awful.

2. Introduce the concept of self-talk as a means of dealing with the negative feelings resulting from negative beliefs. In the example described above, self-talk would involve asking yourself questions such as the following.

   > Is it really so terrible that I can't have the car?

   > Will I die if I don't get it?

   > Just because my parents don't trust me now, does that mean they never will?

   > Why should they let me have the car if I didn't go where I said I would last week?

   Discuss how asking questions of this nature can put the problem in better perspective and reduce the intensity of the feeling.

3. Have students pair up and discuss how they could use self-talk in the examples they identified.

4. Ask volunteers to share examples of the situations and self-talk applications.

Discussion

Content Questions

1. What is self-talk?
2. Was it difficult to think of self-talk examples to apply to your situation?

Personalization Questions

1. Have you ever used a type of self-talk before? If so, what effect did it have on your reactions to the other person involved?
2. How can you apply the concepts from this lesson in your interactions with others?

To the Leader

Initially, students may think that self-talk isn't realistic or that it doesn't make any difference in terms of how they feel. Stress the connection between beliefs and feelings and point out that, if they can talk to themselves and be more realistic about a situation, they may not change the person or the situation, but they can change the degree to which they feel negative.

Depend on Me?

Objective

To distinguish between healthy and unhealthy dependence in relationships

Materials

Paper and pencils as needed

Procedure

1. Discuss the meaning of the word *dependence* (relying on someone for support or aid, being influenced or controlled).

2. Indicate that dependence can be healthy or unhealthy and share an example of each: Healthy dependence might be expecting your boyfriend or girlfriend to provide companionship, whereas unhealthy dependence might be feeling you need that person's acceptance so much that you make yourself available whenever the person wants you to be. Healthy dependence might be relying on a friend for support and encouragement during a stressful time, whereas unhealthy dependence might be relying on that friend to help you make all of your decisions all of the time.

3. Divide students into small groups (3–4 participants) and have them brainstorm examples of healthy and unhealthy dependence.

4. After 10 minutes, invite students to share some examples of each type.

Discussion

Content Questions

1. While you were brainstorming, was it difficult to distinguish between healthy and unhealthy dependence?

2. What are some of the negative results of unhealthy dependence?

Personalization Questions

1. Have you ever been in a relationship in which you felt there was unhealthy dependence? How did you feel about it? Were there any long-term negative effects from this relationship?

2. What do you think you can do to prevent unhealthy dependence in relationships?

To the Leader

Unhealthy dependence in relationships is related to low self-esteem, a high need for approval and acceptance, insecurity, and lack of assertiveness. Students need to recognize that unhealthy dependence can prevent them from acting in their own best interests and that such relationships generally have negative consequences because the dependent person loses self-respect.

I Can't Live without Him/Her

Objective

To differentiate between disappointment and devastation when a relationship terminates

Materials

Paper and pencils as needed

Procedure

1. To introduce the lesson, ask students to think of a popular song, movie, or book in which the theme is "I can't live without you." Generally, this theme occurs when one partner in a relationship has broken up and the other partner feels devastated and doesn't think he or she can go on living.

2. Next discuss reasons students think the person who has been left behind feels so devastated. Discuss the difference between feeling devastated and feeling very disappointed that the relationship ended.

Discussion

Content Questions

1. Do you think devastation or disappointment is the most common feeling when a relationship ends?

2. What could account for the difference between feeling devastated or disappointed? Which do you think is preferable?

Personalization Questions

1. If you have ever felt devastated when a relationship ended, what did you do about your feelings?

2. What do you think you could do to prevent the feeling of devastation?

To the Leader

The feeling of devastation occurs because people tell themselves they are worthless if someone doesn't want to be in a relationship with them, that they will never find anyone else to care about again, or that life isn't worth living. When feelings of devastation occur, people are more likely to feel hopeless and perhaps even consider suicide. Help students recognize the difference between devastation and disappointment and stress that such feelings won't last forever.

What's Desirable?

Objective

To identify characteristics desirable in long-term relationships

Materials

Articles relating to relationship issues (Dear Abby, "Can This Marriage Be Saved?" from *Ladies Home Journal*, etc.); paper and pencils as needed

Procedure

1. Divide students into groups of three and distribute a separate article to each person in each group. Instruct students to read the articles quickly.

2. Next ask them to compare the content of their articles and to discuss, in their groups, characteristics that they think are unhealthy or undesirable and that have resulted in relationship problems for the people involved. For example, perhaps one of the people in the relationship lied to another or perhaps neither person expressed feelings openly.

3. After several minutes, invite groups to share some of their examples. Make a composite list on the chalkboard.

4. Discuss what positive relationship characteristics might correspond to the negative characteristics listed on the board. Write these on the board as well.

Discussion

Content Questions

1. Which characteristics stand out to you as being the most undesirable? Which are the most desirable?

2. Do you think it is possible for any relationship to have all desirable characteristics? How do you decide how many or which undesirable characteristics to tolerate?

3. If you were in a relationship that had a lot of undesirable characteristics, what options would exist for making changes?

4. Is it one person's fault when there are problems in a relationship?

Personalization Questions

1. Have you ever been in a relationship characterized by undesirable or unhealthy characteristics? What was that like for you? Did you feel powerless to change the relationship, or were you able to work on the negative aspects?

2. What do you think you can do in the future to bring about more desirable relationships?

To the Leader

It is important for students to realize that, in relationships, nothing is only one person's fault. Generally, the interaction of the two creates the problems. Recognizing that they can communicate feelings, request change, and commit themselves to working on problems can help students overcome the powerless feeling that often results in unhealthy relationships.

INDEX OF ACTIVITIES

ABOUT THE AUTHOR

Ann Vernon, Ph.D., is an associate professor and coordinator of counseling in the Department of Educational Administration and Counseling at the University of Northern Iowa, Cedar Falls. Dr. Vernon is the director of the Midwest Center for Rational-Emotive Therapy, an affiliate of the Institute for Rational-Emotive Therapy, founded by Dr. Albert Ellis. In addition, she is a therapist in private practice, working primarily with children and their families, and consults with teachers, parents, and mental health professionals on a variety of issues.

Dr. Vernon holds a doctorate in counseling and human development from the University of Iowa and has received advanced training in psychotherapy from the Institute for Rational-Emotive Therapy. She is the author of several emotional education programs for students, including *Help Yourself to a Healthier You* (Minneapolis: Burgess, 1989). Her current research interests focus on rational-emotive education with children, child stress, and consultation.